TRADE AND LETTERS:

Their Journeyings Round the World.

THREE DISCOURSES,

DELIVERED BEFORE THE MERCANTILE LIBRARY ASSOCIATION OF SAN FRANCISCO, AND PUBLISHED AT THE REQUEST OF THE ASSOCIATION.

BY

W. A. SCOTT, D.D.

Homo sum: humani nihil a me alienum puto.—TERENCE.

Etenim omnes artes, quæ ad humanitatem pertinent, habent quoddam commune vinculum, et quasi cognatione quadam inter se continentur.—CIC. PRO ARCH.

NEW YORK:
ROBERT CARTER & BROTHERS,
No. 530 BROADWAY.
1856.

STEREOTYPED BY
THOMAS B. SMITH,
82 & 84 Beekman-street.

PRINTED BY
E. O. JENKINS,
24 Frankfort-st.

Dedication.

TO

THE MEMBERS

OF THE

MERCANTILE LIBRARY ASSOCIATION

OF SAN FRANCISCO.

In dedicating this little volume to you, gentlemen, I seek to do honor to myself by recording the distinction you have conferred upon me by inviting me to lecture before you, and by expressing your approbation of my humble efforts. "What is writ is writ," but for your sakes, as well as for the cause, "I would it were worthier."

Yours, very respectfully,

W. A. SCOTT.

San Francisco, 10*th May*, 1856.

CONTENTS.

LECTURE I.

HOMES OF TRADE AND LETTERS.

LECTURE II.

TRADE AND LETTERS; THEIR CONNECTION AND INFLUENCE ON THE PROGRESS OF NATIONS.

LECTURE III.

HINTS ON THE COMMERCIAL SPIRIT OF THE AGE.

APPENDIX.

A.

THE ARMY OF THE WAREHOUSE.

B.

REPUBLICS AND LETTERS.

C.

COMMERCE CONQUERING.

D.

CRADLE OF OUR RACE.

E.

CARTHAGE.

F.

ACCURACY OF OLD WRITERS.

G.

ANTIQUITY OF COMMERCE.

H.

AUSTRALIA.

I.

J.

MOHAMMED.

K.

GOD IN TRADE.

L.

M.

N.

PREJUDICE AGAINST TRADE UNREASONABLE AND WICKED.

O.

LORENZO DE MEDICI.

P.

CONSCIENCE IN BUSINESS.

LECTURE I.

I.

HOMES OF TRADE AND LETTERS.*

"The extreme regions of the habitable world have received the fairest gifts of nature."—HERODOTUS' "THALIA."

WHILE the Anglican and Roman crosses are leagued with the Crescent against the Greek cross—Britain and Gaul now united to uphold the Turk whom they together sought to destroy when in the twelfth century their banners were last borne to the battle-field in concert; while Europe and Western Asia are shaking under the tramp of bannered hosts, and the bright blue waters of the Black and Baltic Seas are stirred with the keel of ponderous battle-ships, and are echoing with the murderous thunderings of Sinope and Odessa; here at the Golden Gate—the great western gate of this vast continent, so far westward that it looks boldly on the face of the jeweled East—very different, more useful, and more glorious results are being achieved. It was a proud and happy day for America, when California, like Minerva, was born fully grown—

* Lecture delivered before the Mercantile Library Association of San Francisco in Musical Hall, 16th June, 1854.

and with the commerce of the great Pacific, the new and long-sought highway to the Indies, forming the last link in the belt of civilized enterprise which now clasps the world, and when with her rich valleys and golden mountains, from the glittering snows of the Shasta to the burning deserts of the Colorado, she was declared a new State in the confederacy, under the flag of Constitutional Liberty and Representative Republicanism. In the Holy Land the hills may be "everlasting," but they are not so here. This metropolis of commerce in its antecedents and prospects is absolutely without a parallel in the history of cities and nations. Here the rough places are made smooth, and the mountains are made plains. And instead of sand-hills, luxurious houses, marble palaces, and costly marts have risen up. Here I see the surplus waters of one of the most magnificent bays on the globe conquered, and long lines of wharves stretched out, burdened with the rich and useful products of all climes, and noble ships, wearing the crest of every nation, locked to them, or resting on their bosom. A busy, adventurous, enterprising population throng your thoroughfares, exhibiting the complexion and costumes of many different lands. And with wealth and intellect, and a bold, daring spirit, I see here the taste, the refinement and elevation of character, mental and moral, that ennoble the best portions of our older States. And all this, where some five or six years ago, there were no buildings better than cane huts, hide houses, or canvas cabins. Here I see the loftier, as well as the grosser, pursuits of man, encouraged. Here I find private and public schools, equal to those of any country, and temples for the service of the living God with freedom to worship Him. Here are established associations of Christian young men, lyceums and libraries, scientific, benevolent, and literary institutions, and a monthly periodical conducted with marked ability, whose contributors are, I believe, all your own citizens. Here I find a newspaper press, which, in excellence of style and matter, in tone and ability, has astonished me more than almost any other thing in California, which is itself a land of wonders, and an enigma not only to *The Times*, the great thunderer of London, but to the civilized world. And if the actual exports and the prospective commerce of this city—when the great road to the Atlantic shall have been built—and when the wealth of China and Japan, and the islands of the sea shall be poured into your lap, and thence distributed over this entire continent, and to western Europe—when the growth of the Pacific States shall have as far outrun our present conceptions, as the actualities of California have surpassed the anticipations of 1847 and 1849; if, in view of all these things, San Francisco is the TYRE, so when we look at her public spirit, and her early devotion to public schools and literary institutions, we rejoice to hail her also as the ATHENS of the Pacific. It was with some such thoughts as these, that I have ventured to accept your invitation to lecture in behalf of the Mercantile Library Association, and to offer some thoughts on the RISE, GROWTH, AND INFLUENCE OF GREAT CITIES AS THE HOME OF TRADE AND LETTERS.

I. Ours is not an age of iron, nor of brass, nor of gold, though we are distinguished for our use of the useful and precious metals. It is on the contrary, pre-eminently the age of machinery, and of city building, and ocean traveling. The history of the rise and influence of the great cities of our globe is the history of the emergency of our race in each section of our planet, from barbarism into civilization—and of course the history of the rise and progress, power and fall of nations. Zoan, Memphis, Saïs, Thebes, Babylon, Persepolis, Tyre, Carthage, Athens and Rome were great cities; but the earth has never been so full, nor society so thoroughly pervaded with the spirit connatural to great cities, as at the present time. Truly gold is

> "Hoarded, bartered, bought and sold,
> Stolen, borrowed, squandered, doled;
> Price of many a crime untold;"

but still gold is not the only thought of mankind. There are other pursuits and other ambitions than those of filthy lucre. The spirit that now broods over society has grown by slow degrees, and in the midst of great difficulties; but it has eliminated itself from one prison hold after another, until its presence is nearly commensurate with that of our race. Modern civilization owes its extension to commercial enterprise, and modern commerce in its rise and progress is chiefly indebted to the powerful awakening of the human mind at the period of the Crusades, and afterward by the great Reformation of the sixteenth century, and to the subsequent efforts of the Christian world for the evangelization of heathen nations.

The tendency of modern society is toward building large towns and cities. This tendency is apparent even in our newest States, but is seen more palpably in the older ones, and on the continent of Europe, where the people may be said to hardly live in the country at all. This city-building tendency is both cause and consequence of agricultural extension. It discovers itself in the more general recognition of human rights acknowledged in our day, and which is a starting-point in all the movements of modern society, and which has eminently contributed to the influence of congregated masses. Great cities have infused into modern society an impulse to freedom and refinement, and a spirit that eminently favors equality of rights, and full, and fair, and free opportunities for improvement, and for the pursuit and enjoyment of human happiness. The opening of the race of life equally to all classes of men, and the universal diffusion of knowledge and power is the great object of the society that now is, and will be still more the great object of the ages to come. Twice has our race been indebted to cities for civilization and civil liberty. *First*, with the rise of cities, civilization and political institutions began, and, *secondly*, in and by them were developed the principles of independence, self-government, and equal rights in the middle ages. In the Bible we are told Cain dwelt in the land of Nod, on the east of Eden, and built a city, and called it after the name of his son, Enoch. It is strange that the first man who shed the blood of his brother should have been the first builder of cities. Civilization, you know, is a word that comes from *civis*, a citizen, and *civis* is a citizen because he dwells in a city; and in this way, Cain is the founder of civilization subsequent to the expulsion from Eden. The origin of cities certainly belongs to the earliest period of history.

Relationship, man's innate love for society, the necessity of defense against wild beasts and more powerful neighbors, together with purposes of traffic, led first to permanent settlements. The two great objects of cities in ancient times were safety and trade. If security was the object, then the site selected was generally the slope or summit of some lofty rock, as is seen to this day in the sites of the old castles of the Rhine. If trade was the object, then the bank of some large river, or the head of some bay of the sea, having a rich back country, was selected as the site for the city's foundation. In the latter case, as security for life and property was necessary for trade, so art and labor were required to provide the means of defense, in the shape of massive walls, and strong military towers. As the population of these communities increased, so their wants and consequent trade, skill and available force multiplied. The great capitals of Egypt and Asia were situated on the banks of their principal rivers, and defended by extraordinary works of art. In a commercial and military point of view, there is scarcely on the globe a more eligible position than this. I should say but one, and that is Constantinople, the prize now so eagerly sought by the great powers of the world. The All-wise Creator, in his munificence, has marked out this place as the site of a great city.

II. Ancient cities may also be classed as either military, as Sparta and Rome, or commercial, as Tyre and Carthage, or mixed, as Memphis, Thebes, Babylon, and Nineveh. In all of these there was a blending together, more or less, of the arts of war and peace. The cities of Egypt, Assyria, and Greece were both marts of commerce, and centers of vast military power. And even in ancient times, if *commerce* was not then king, still it was more powerful and long-lived than despotism. Empires rose and fell with astounding rapidity. But the machinery of commerce outlived the enginery of war. Military rule often rose as a mushroom, and perished in a night; but companies of peaceful merchants such as are described in oriental tales, continued to pace their way from one caravansera to another, alike regardless whether Pharaoh, Sesostris, or Nebuchadnezzar sat upon the throne. They were but little affected by the change of one dynasty for another. The great military roads of Babylon, stretching from the Persian Gulf to the Ægæan Sea, and from the Nile to the Oxus, were used as the highways of merchants long after the soldiers of the golden empire had ceased to traverse them. Whether the last conqueror were the "barbarian shepherd king," or the more civilized Mede, all were sagacious enough to perceive that the wealth and power of empires must be derived mainly from the ingenuity and enterprise of commerce; and accordingly they did not fail to protect and encourage the productive skill and extending trade of their dominions. The same remarks are true of the Roman roads and of the policy of the Cæsars. The cities of Phenicia in their day, were to the known world what the manufacturing and commercial cities of Europe and the United States are now to the nations of the globe.

Homer sung of their arts and of their enterprise. For many centuries they were the great discoverers both by land and sea; their navigators were found upon every known water, and their wares were exposed for sale in every market, and bartered in every recess and hovel of barbarism. Similar was the trade of the cities of Arabia Felix, with the empires and people between the Hellespont and Cape Comorin. Africa and Asia also were their neighbors, and with them they carried on constant commercial intercourse. And the result was, that the narrow strip of the great Arabian peninsula where this great commercial people dwelt, from being a wilderness became a garden, and their houses and public buildings were adorned with the works of art like palaces, whose ruins are now visited among the greatest wonders of the world. By means of their commerce they derived wealth and civilization from the older and more powerful nations, and the looms and dyes of Babylon outvied the power of her kings. The cities of Egypt and Asia, however, knew nothing of the institutions of popular intelligence and suffrage, which at a later period adorned ancient Greece, and now, with a thousandfold increased influence, vigor, and purity, pervade a portion of Europe and America. Even oriental merchant cities possessed very little of the principle of self-government. In passing through their streets, the largest mass of people to be seen were slaves engaged in the labors of city traffic, and offices of domestic servitude. Mixed with these were a few country farmers, selling their produce. The luxuries, the wealth, the refinement, and the power were in the hands of a few. Tyre had but little foreign commerce, but was a great manufactory. Holy Scripture informs us that king Solomon sent year by year to that city, twenty thousand measures of wheat, and twenty measures of pure oil, in exchange for firs and cedars. Its inhabitants were merchants, priests, soldiers and sovereigns, with weavers, traders and workmen, donkeys, dogs, and camels; yet she was "filled with wisdom, and understanding, and cunning to work all works of brass."

III. Commerce, manufactures, and agriculture, have, in a great measure, taken the place of feudal wars, and semi-barbarous fêtes. The feudal and the military have given place to the commercial and civic. For several centuries the forms and the spirit which characterize modern society, have been making their way into the place of those which were characteristic of society in the middle ages. In Europe, the ancient and modern states of society are represented by the landlord class, and the mercantile class. Aristocracy, royalty, and church establishments, supported by the State, are the incorporation of what remains of the form and spirit of remote times. And in no part of Europe is the struggle between the feudal and the civic, so prevailing, so organized, and so determined as in England. In no other Protestant country are there so many and so great inconsistencies, and such palpable contrasts as in Great Britain. In no other country is there so great wealth, luxury, intelligence, and magnificence, in such close proximity with ignorance, degradation, and vice. Great Britain is incomparably the greatest, richest, best-governed nation in Europe; yet it were difficult to find greater depravity, ignorance, and vice on the globe, than prevails in the streets of Glasgow and London. In no other Protestant country is there so great a hierarchy, and so wealthy, intelligent, numerous, and powerful an aristocracy; and in no part of the globe, except in our own country, is there a commercial power embodying so fully the spirit of the age, as in England. And every fresh accession to the strength of the commercial party, becomes the occasion of a deeper jealousy and of a more active hostility on the side of the parties adhering to the ancient order of things. Every new spinning jenny, and locomotive, and ton of railroad iron that is ordered from the shops and warehouses of England, is an addition to the modern spirit of society. Lord Brougham said in his remarkably able speech in 1811, on the "Order in Council"—"Circumstanced as the two countries are, I use no figure of speech, but state the simple fact, when I say, that not an ax falls in the woods of America which does not put in motion some shuttle, or hammer, or wheel in England." (P. 454, vol. i., Speeches.) There is at every great era of the history of the world, a leading principle, which gives direction to the fortunes of nations, and the characters of distinguished men. This principle in our times, is that of the action and re-action upon each other of Europe and America, for the advancement of free institutions, and the promotion of national liberty. Ever since the discovery of America, this principle has been in operation, but naturally and necessarily with vastly increased energy, since the growth of an intelligent population on this side of the Atlantic. The restlessness of our times, and the fierceness of party strife — even the murmurings of one nation against another, is evidence of healthful activity. Where there is no life, there will be no movement. The strugglings and overactings of some portions of modern society, is evidence of the depths of its breathings. They are signs of life, struggling to throw off some unhealthy accretions, but of life that is youthful and vigorous. Where there is great vigor, there will be action, and thinking, and diversity of opinion, both as to what should be done, and the best method of doing it. The many months that our legislators spend making speeches at so much per diem, are not lost. It is a great blessing to the country.

It is a great relief to the gentlemen themselves to be delivered of superfluous excitement, and it is necessary to their constituents. It will sometimes happen that a multitude of words darkens counsel; but generally by much speaking is much light. Not a speech is lost. It has its mission to fulfill. A man's neighbors will read *his* speech, when they will not read any thing else. And I should reckon it a something gained for society, if every American constituent should read one speech a year, even if it were made for Bunkum. For it can not be conceived that any speech could be read without exciting a thought of some kind, and the simple exciting of any mind to the perpetration of a thought is an impulse toward something better. Wherever there is *thinking*, there is hope of improvement. I am decidedly in favor of legislators making speeches to their constituents, even if the reporter writes them. Any thing that agitates the mass of mind—that leads the people to think, to read, to examine, and to act for themselves, is of vast moment in such a country as ours. It is only under a despotism that men can neither move nor mutter. It is under such a government that all public feeling and popular intelligence are smothered to death, and the people are left sitting, *quietly*, it may be, but it is the quietness of dejection, the sullenness of despair, the lethargy of death. There is no paradox in saying that the most captious, hard to please, grumbling nation, is, after all, the most moral and the most free. In spite of the contempt which Napoleon sought to cast upon Great Britain, when he called her a "nation of shop-keepers," his loftiest efforts of genius were directed toward the pulling down of those shops, the arresting of her looms, and the crippling of her commerce, and in the fruitless but most gigantic scheme to make Antwerp the London of the world. And never was there a moment when the commercial interests of England were so great as at present, and never was her wealth, power, influence, and domestic happiness greater. The growth of her great cities is the result of her commerce; and her commerce is the result of her home industry, skill in machinery, and enterprise in trade; and these agencies in turn have built her large towns, which, in their turn, operate upon the intelligence, agriculture, manufactures, morals, and piety of the nation. It is because Great Britain is the HOME of great cities, that she is the greatest commercial power on the globe, and is secure in the possession of her greatness in nearly all other respects. So glorious is the progress of knowledge, so triumphant the onward progress of civil liberty, so diffusive the spirit of Christianity, and so broad the base of modern civilization, that the shadows of coming events of good things are already descending upon the nations of the earth. The spirit of our age will have its way. There will be no retrocession in the march of revolutions, however much the sun may seem to go back on the dial of freedom. A band of iron is making which is to be welded, and hold within its circle a world with no other conflicts but those of genius, and no weapons but those of honest rivalry, and no institutions but those of freedom and Christianity.

For weal or woe, a revolution in favor of the commercial and civic states of society has been begun, that can never go back. And of this revolution cities are the palpable flesh and blood, or at least the brick and mortar embodiments. They are the triumphal columns of the victory of liberal principles over the rudeness and military power of feudal ages, and the priestly arts of the debasing superstitions of former times. The jealousy, envy, and prejudices then that would blot them out of existence as but little better than concretions of ignorance, vice, and irreligion—and that would remove them from the body politic as "unsightly wens," belong to the little, one-sided, one-eyed, narrow, contracted, mean, and pusillanimous spirit of the semi-barbarous ages that have long since gone down the sky to the regions of eternal night.

It was once happily said by Burke, whose eloquence and wit were surpassed only by his learning and philosophy, when pleading for the parks and public squares of London against the littleness of soul and the greediness of avarice that sought to convert them into shops and warehouses: "that they were the lungs of London, and the Thames its great artery." Keeping up the figure, we would say, great cities are the lungs of modern society, and steam navigation its great artery. Large towns are the breathing apparatus of the last and best forms of civilization.

Philosophy teaches us that the broader the base of a pillar, the stronger the foundation, and the higher the apex of the shaft may rise. On this rule, then, we can not doubt as to the permanence of Republican Institutions, and the complete triumph of the great principles infused into modern society by Christianity. "The area of freedom" is becoming so wide—the base of modern civilization so broad, that nothing short of the annihilation of a large part of our race, and the total oblivion of man's noblest achievements for six thousand years, can drive mankind back to the darkness and despotism of former ages. Time was when civilization was confined to Jews, Egyptians, Greeks or Romans; and when their country fell respectively beneath the stroke of barbarians, then civilization was well-nigh blotted out from the world. But it is not so now. If, by any revolution of things, Europe should go back to skins and acorns, the monkey-like Paradise state of the human race, that so much delights some of our *savans;* and if St. Petersburg should be sacked and given to the plunder of the Turk; if Vienna, Paris and London should fall into ruins and become as Thebes, Palmyra, and Nineveh now are, still America would be left for the preservation of arts and arms, commerce and religion. And if America should be tossed by civil commotions or endangered by the invasions of hostile and barbarous foes, her children embodying the spirit of their fathers, as the seed for new generations, would take up their abode in the islands of the sea, bearing with them their civilization and arts, as Æneas bore old Anchises from the walls of burning Troy. In spite of kingcraft and priestcraft, of ignorance and despotism, of earth and hell, I believe in the ever onward, upward, hopeful view of our race. The highest form of human civilization, and the most perfect state of civil liberty, is that in which man was created—in the image and after the likeness of the ever-blessed God—and as the Gospel prevails and restores man to that image, so the base of true freedom will become as wide as the world, and its top shall reach unto heaven—to the throne of the Eternal—and the angels of God will come down to sing the pæans of universal victory over selfishness, bigotry, ignorance and oppression, in the temple built by Liberty's devotees.

IV. Notwithstanding the present war of the great nations, the commercial spirit is gaining over the warlike.

The producer is superseding the destroyer. Peace hath had her heroes no less than war. A half century ago, causes more trifling than the marriage of Louis Napoleon would have produced a war between England and France. The fishery question, the boundary question, the Sandwich Islands, the Mosquito kingdom, Cuba, the *Black Warrior* affair, and the costume regulations of the Secretary of State, would have plunged us into war before this, but for the influence of commercial interests.* Such is the progress of freedom in thought, and in government, and in trade, and so large the liberality of sentiment characteristic of our times, that the army of the warehouse prevails over the army of the bayonet. The ledger of Christian counting houses, express offices and insurance companies, is converting the sword into the plowshare. The power of the feudal lord has paled before the intelligence of the Christianized farmer. But as the forest is subdued, and agriculture advances, and commerce increases, and nations are bonded together by intercourse and trade, so will ships multiply and roads be constructed, and large towns grow up, and the inhabitants of our globe be emancipated from political and social vassalage.

Philosophers, and cabinets, and monarchs, are beginning to see that science is lending her influence in many powerful forms for effecting this great result. The new

* See Appendix A.

and speedy communication between great cities in Europe and Asia, and between Europe and Asia and America, will necessarily tend to swell the large towns into still greater magnitude, and to diminish the weight of the smaller intervening places, and the social influence of the country population. Every-where, in Europe and America, there is a prevailing disposition to converge upon great points. Large towns are increasing in number, and absorbing all the smaller within their vicinity. Investments in villages and small towns are so hazardous that they have nothing better than a nominal value. This may be unwise and perilous, but it is so, nor do we see the slightest prospect of a change, nor do we believe that it will ever be otherwise for any considerable period of time.

Modern Europe is the offspring of the feudal system that grew up amidst the ruins of ancient civilization. The transition of power from the hands of the victims of corrupt civilization to the ruder but stronger grasp of the Northern barbarians, produced but little change on the towns and cities of Europe. The spirit of popular liberty, inherent in the Gothic institutions of the new settlers, readily blended with something of the former policy and jurisprudence. The bonds of society were soon so far replaced that life and health began slowly to return. During the darkest ages, something of social refinement and of the elements of improvement remained in the large towns and cities, and in the eleventh and twelfth centuries, came the practice of granting charters to boroughs and cities, and from that time the principles of self-government in our municipal system became more defined, more fully recognized, and better understood. The Romans built colonial cities in Gaul, Africa, Spain, Germany and Switzerland, under Augustus and his predecessors, many of which exist to this day. Charlemagne, from a strong desire to civilize the Germans, and cement his empire together, compelled many of them to live in cities. Henry the First distinguished himself so much on account of his zeal in building cities, and granting them privileges, that he has been called *Henry the city builder.* The power and growth of the cities broke down the feudal system. In many of the large cities, castles were erected to protect the inhabitants, and the cruel oppression of feudal laws, and wandering knights and robbers, drove many of the peasants to reside in cities. This gave rise to greater trade and to the cultivation of the various arts within their walls. And as several neighboring lords sometimes leagued together for the subjugation of a city, so cities sometimes leagued together to resist their attacks, and the result of the contest was generally in favor of a popular government. The people of such towns, choosing their own rulers, retaining their own keys, and enacting their own laws, soon began to understand the doctrine of self-government, and the principles of representation—a principle that had no place in the free governments of antiquity. As early as the reign of Edward III., English boroughs were deemed of sufficient importance to send members to Parliament, along with the knights of the shield, and both sat together, constituting conjointly, the second house of the British legislature. Not less than seventy times during his reign were the representatives of boroughs assembled with the knights in a legislative capacity. There was, however, but a feeble approach in the Amphyctionic council and the Achæan league of the Greeks, to any thing like the representative system of the British House of Commons, and the Republican Representation of the Congress of the United States.

As the immediate object of commerce is gain, commercial states are always reluctant to engage in war. All the glory of all the victories to be gained by the combined fleets and armies of France and England will not satisfy the merchants of those countries. So intimate and philosophical is the connection between commerce and political freedom, that it is not too much to say, that the treasure, as well as the blood of our ancestors, is the price of our liberties. The principles of independence and self-government ascend from the city to the

Senate; from the chamber of commerce to the heads of the departments of the State and of the Treasury. The more fully and intelligibly the principles of independence and self-government are acted upon in the towns and cities of a nation, the more generally will the people become interested in its affairs, and the greater is the probability that statesmen will regulate their conduct by principles that will abide the severest scrutiny. When the *spirit* and *forms* of constitutional liberty are *localized* in neighborhoods and cities, we have the best possible guaranty against their being *centralized* at the seat of government. "It has been found necessary," says Curran in his speech on the election of Lord Mayor of Dublin in 1770, "to establish at least some few incorporated bodies, to serve as great depositories of popular strength." In Great Britain he informs us the importance of such repositories has long been understood, and "hoarded up with the wisest forecast and preserved with a religious reverence as an unfailing resource against those times of storm, in which it is the will of Providence that all human affairs should sometimes fluctuate; and as such, they have been found at once a protection to the people, and a security to the government." The intelligence and social virtue of localized forms of popular government in cities, seems to serve the same purposes of protection and security both for the people and the general government, that a nucleus of a few thousand regular soldiers do for the formation, discipline, encouragement, and comfort of new volunteers.

The errors of enlightened and free cities in matters of general government, if err they should, are only specks that arise for a moment upon the surface of a splendid luminary; consumed by its own heat, or irradiated by its own light, they soon disappear, as our cities soon renew themselves after the ravages of a fire; but the perverseness of an uneducated mass of mean and narrow intellect, without social habits and the kindly humanizing effects of close and intimate society, are like the excrescences that grow upon a body naturally cold and dark—no fire to waste them, and no ray to enlighten; they assimilate and coalesce with those qualities congenial to their nature, and acquire an incorrigible permanence in their union with kindred frost, and kindred opacity. It is only where men are congregated in masses, and are subjected to the stimulus of each others' sympathies and rivalries, and are brought under the influence of discipline and social virtues, and the humanizing effects of civilization, and the refinements of education and wealth, that they have opinions worth contending about, and that the great questions belonging to good government find their birthplace and advance toward maturity.

"By mutual confidence and mutual aid
Great deeds are done, and great discoveries made,
The wise, new prudence from the wise acquire,
And one brave hero fans another's fire."—POPE'S HOMER.

V. If the designs of Providence in regard to great cities can be learned from their history and influence on their respective territories, it is clear that they are powerful AGENTS for whatever Providence has designed man to do upon earth. Human agency is necessary to keep the earth from degenerating into a monstrous wilderness, fruitful in every rank production, and every unclean thing. In the command, then, to multiply and fill the earth, and till the land, was included a command to build cities. The wandering hordes of Mongolians and Tartars spread over the vast flats of Central Asia, from earliest times to the present, and the aborigines of Germany, Great Britain, and America, and the Indians of your own mountains are examples of what man is, and what he will be, without cities. The ancient people of God, in Judea, and ancient Egypt, Phenicia, Greece, and Rome, with their arms, arts, and letters, and modern Europe, and the populous educated States of America, are examples of what men are, and may become under the humanizing and elevating influence of great cities. So dependent is man upon a combination of social agencies for means to diminish the inquietudes and discomforts of a rude and uncivilized state, and to procure peace and enjoyment for himself, that he is incapable of realizing his high destiny without associations with his fellow-man.

> "God, working ever on the social plan,
> By various ties attaches man to man."

The habit and capability of enjoying the romance and seclusion and repose of the country, is usually derived from the busy scenes of life. It is the education of the city which man has built that gives us power to observe and opens up the susceptibilities of the heart to the country God has made. We are now prepared, I trust, to say, in the next place,

VI. THAT THE INFLUENCE OF CITIES ON POLITICAL SCIENCE IS VERY GREAT. To some extent this has been anticipated in what has been said of the rise, early history, and constitution of cities. The first form of government was patriarchal. As families enlarged, and the heads of family-states died, it became necessary to ELECT a chief, and thus political institutions began to assume a systematic character.

As purposes of trade and defense of life and property caused men to build cities and surround them with walls without, so necessity soon taught them to make laws within. And the very first division of labor and distinction between *meum* and *tuum*, produced some idea of equal rights and of personal independence and self-respect. And the intercourse of these towns, one with another, called for laws and tribunals of justice, and a kind of international code, and a desire for refinement and reputation were the natural results. And as these salutary consequences were enjoyed, the idea of self-reliance, of independence, of home, and of the love of country would naturally be developed. And as a municipal body, every city soon had its local regulations, and its local functionaries. These regulations, and the powers of these functionaries emanating from the people, were expressions of the popular will. And thus a popular character was very soon and very naturally attached to the municipal law and authority of great cities. They became *imperia in imperia.* And such, in a great degree, they are still. In all past ages, and in all countries, whether in Asia, Africa, Europe or America, where the people have attained any thing like free institutions, and achieved a high degree of wealth, and consequently of civilization, it is found that there were built great cities, and that in them were concentrated and longest preserved the elements of civilization and freedom.

Heeren has justly remarked, that "the rise of cities was the most important source of the Republicanism of antiquity." This was particularly true of Greece. And Lord Brougham has said that "the manufactures and commerce of England give life and vigor to the main pillars of liberty in the realm." Speeches, vol. i., p. 457, Edinburgh edition.

The necessities of city governments are of a strong Republican tendency. The cities of Italy are to this day the most important remnants of the great fabric of ancient civilization. It was amid their bloody contests with one another, that they lighted the torch of modern civilization. It was the cities of Northern Italy that opened the way for the progress of improvement, by confederating together against the Emperors of Germany, very much as the most important cities of Greece entered into a confederation to oppose the power of Macedon. The Achæan and the Hanseatic leagues, and the confederacy of the High German and Rhenish cities from the foot of the Alps to the mouth of the Mayne in 1253, and of the Suabian cities in 1488, and more recent commercial unions and treaties will suggest something to your minds of their immense influence on human affairs. Time peremptorily forbids me to enter on the history of confederate cities, and I am sorry to say, I do not know of any good history in our language on the rise and influence of free cities.*

VII. Let us consider next the INFLUENCE OF CITIES ON PHYSICAL SCIENCE. And what are the monuments of

* See Appendix M.

Thebes and Persepolis, of Athens and Rome, but the "mutilated treatises" of the ancients on science? Their monuments, like their literature, are memorials of their minds, showing us their developments of thought, reasoning, imagination, and truth. Cities are known to us as once having existed great in power and wealth, not so much from their preserved written literature, as by the moldering fragments of their science. It is thus with Copan, Uxmal, Palenque, Etruria, Petra, and the cities of the Nile and Euphrates. Every region of country that has become the seat of a great city, has become the HOME of an improved agriculture. This results in part from the wealth of cities, and in part from their mechanical and scientific skill. Do not the associations of the city fell the forest, build the aqueduct and canal, drain the swamp, and open up highways of travel and trade?

The Babylonians, the Carthaginians, the Moslems of Spain, and the nations of modern Europe are scarcely less celebrated for the adorning of their capitals than for the agricultural improvements of their respective territories. Lands nearest great cities are more valuable than those remote, and the larger the city, the more valuable the land in its neighborhood. Large portions of the earth's surface is not fit for cultivation until it is cleared and drained, and this requires means, money, and skill, which the city alone can furnish. I know it is said that commercial States are selfish and mercenary. If so, how does it happen that Great Britain and the United States are at the same time both the most benevolent and commercial nations on the globe? How does it happen that sufferers by flood and fire, by robbery and tyranny in all parts of the world—from the cry of the Greeks to the refugees of political proscription in 1848—have shared our almsgivings? Where was it, and whence but from the great marts of commerce, a hundred thousand dollars flowed into the treasury of the Howards during the prevalence of the epidemic of last summer in my own city?* And how is it that, according to a well-informed newspaper, the amount of money raised in the United States and sent abroad within the last forty-five years for charitable purposes, far exceeds the amount due to Europe for interest on all the debts of all the States of the Union? And where, but in our large towns and cities, are the funds obtained to build churches, colleges, and asylums?

It is said again, that a city population is fickle and superficial—that they are "like Zimri, all things by fits and starts, and nothing long." It may be that the mass of the city are superficial thinkers, and do not achieve profound scholarship. They may not excel in brilliant emanations of intellect; but, still a commercial people are always an ingenious, quick witted people. A commercial age is also

* New Orleans.

a deep-thinking age. And if the deep-thinking is not done in the city, it is encouraged, supported, and directed by the city. The cities of a trading people are the forges and workshops of thought—deep, powerful, upheaving, deathless thought. The profound thinkings of a commercial people may not be committed to paper in Parnassian rythm, nor in Ciceronian periods. Its vehicle of communication with the outer world is more generally a series of Arabic abstractions called figures, which soon assume local habitations and names for the most substantial comforts and highest pursuits and enjoyments of man. It is true that every one that has money to purchase fine pictures and statuary, has not the taste of a Reynolds, a West, a Canova, or a Powers. All men are not equally able for all things. But an admiration for the fine arts argues good taste. If

> "To dally much with subjects mean and low
> Proves that the mind is weak, or makes it so,"

then the disposition to patronize the higher departments of letters and arts, is proof of a refined judgment and an elevated taste. If the embellishing of the houses, halls, temples and public institutions of cities, and the residences of merchant princes, supports the artist; if it is the use of the wealth of the city that creates the taste and furnishes the means for the enjoyment of pictures and statues; if it is the demand that calls forth the supply, then it will be found, that it is from the emporiums of trade that the mandate issues to send Nature forth

> "To teach the canvas innocent deceit,
> Or lay the landscape on the snowy sheet."

If the city gives value and beauty to the fields and gardens of the country, and tames the stubborn soil and makes it fruitful, and furnishes a market for its products, and builds and adorns the landlord's palace, much more does it improve and elevate his taste to the possession and enjoyment of the works of art. If all the world were farmers they might have bread and beef enough, but the mass of mankind would be idle, untaught and narrow-minded. For it is the excitement of trade, the conflicts of a generous rivalry, and the enlargement of ideas consequent upon the exchange of the products of one country for those of another, that call forth the powers of the mind and the heart, that gathering wealth and social comforts expand into civilization.

Wealth, that is the comforts that wealth commands, has a tendency to improve the general health and prolong the mean duration of human life, and health and long life in their turn produce wealth. They are mutually cause and consequence—both the results of advancing civilization, and both contributing every hour to carry on civilization to a yet higher point of excellence. History proves that wealth and knowledge combined have done much to prevent human casualties, and have generated a nature favorable to a healthy physical condition of society alike calculated to ward off the attacks of disease and to baffle them when they are incurred. Philosophers, physicians and educators have been successful in awakening the public mind to the vast importance of the proper ventilation of sitting-rooms, sleeping chambers, and school-houses, and the wicked absurdities of whalebones and thin soled shoes. A French writer has shown that persons of high rank have better health and live longer than those that are subjected to pain, anxiety and hard labor—that the middle class far exceed the poor in health and length of life. The cultivation of the mind, whether from direct intuition, or from improved social circumstances, or from a combination of these and other causes, increases the mental power both to endure and to enjoy. The officers of the grand army of Napoleon stood out longer than the privates in the retreat from Moscow, although the previous habits of both parties would seem to have indicated the very reverse. The same observation is true of our army in Mexico. Literary men, and artisans, and clergymen, in Europe and in this country, who have a competence, are long-lived in their generation. The insurance offices of England show that of the middle classes who have insured their lives, the annual average of mortality compared with that of the negro slaves of the British West Indies from 1800 to 1820, was one to eighty-one, while that of the negroes was one to every five or six. As the wealth and domestic comforts of Europe and America have increased, so has the average duration of life increased, and the ratio of mortality diminished.

Statistical inquiries in this country have scarcely begun, and in Europe they have hardly reached the maturity of a science; yet they are so far advanced as to enable life insurance companies to operate with perfect safety. And it were a blessing in the advancement of civilization, if the foolish prejudices that still exist against life insurance offices were all overcome, and our salaried men, mechanics, clerks and packers, laborers and draymen who are married—and they all ought to be married, and to have their wives with them in California—if they all invested a portion of their income every month as a deposit for their families in Life Insurances.

The influence of cities upon the fine arts is seen in the fact, that the adornments of the castles of Europe were borrowed from its merchant palaces. Germany and Flanders, Genoa and Venice, excited the envy of the feudal aristocracy, and then military nobles and scions of royal blood began to cultivate a taste for the fine arts. It is an undenied matter of fact, that the revival of the fine arts in Europe, was much more the work of its merchants than of its nobles or of its princes. It is not an aristocracy of privilege and blood, but of wealth and genius that creates and fosters the fine arts, and when they shall cease to have the patronage of the trader and the citizen, then they will perish from the face of the earth. Along with the skill that produces, comes the means of possession and the capacity to enjoy. The Republican traders of Holland had a fine school of art a hundred years before the aristocracy of England could boast a single one.* But as England has become great in commerce and in building cities, so has her tastes for the fine arts improved also. And the English art of the nineteenth century is just such an improvement upon the Dutch school, as English naval power and commercial greatness surpass that of Holland in the seventeenth century. The pictures and statues and histories of Greece that surrounded the Roman youth, educated them to be the men they were, just as the atmosphere of the Alleghany makes the strong mountaineer. This, then, should teach us to have public Squares, Fountains and Statuary, Libraries, Lyceums, Museums and Fairs for the people. It is by the presence of such things a healthful public taste may be created.

* See Appendix B.

FINALLY. The more commercial and town building States have always been in the van of POPULAR EDUCATION. This was true of Holland and Spain in their glory, and is now eminently true of OLD and NEW ENGLAND. It is not my purpose to enter upon an examination of the difference between the state of education in agricultural and mining districts, compared with those of the manufacturing districts of Europe, nor to consider the state of popular education in large towns and cities, in contradistinction to that of rural districts; but it is believed that such an examination would show a vast result in favor of manufacturing districts and cities—both as to the *number* of schools and their *efficiency*, and as to the number of children receiving instruction and the proficiency of their studies—nor can I now compare the state of education in America with that of Europe, although when abroad in the old world, I made some examination into the condition of European schools, and the result is that I am more than ever satisfied that American schools and systems of education and elementary books and training are in every respect, except that of physical education, worthy to be compared with the best in Europe. And in some respects, especially in activity of mental habits, universality of attainments, and adaptedness to the nature of free institutions and the useful pursuits of life, I consider our schools superior to any in the world. There is a healthfulness and a purity and modesty, and a vigor in the mass of the people in our oldest and best regulated communities, that can not be found abroad. Our free institutions as they emanate from the Federal Constitution and from Washington, and are possessed by our sovereign States and in municipal bodies, and especially as they are connected with the two dearest rights of man, the *liberty of the Press* and the *liberty of conscience*, contribute to render our country a scene of constant mental training. Though our territory is immensely large and our population widely scattered, yet such is our mobility, our intercourse and activity, our traveling and intercommunion one State with another, and one city with another, and of the country with the city, and so universal the circulation of newspapers and the diffusion of the blessings of education, that substantially all our large towns and populous districts enjoy the advantages of a city population, with a freer circulation of pure air. The newspapers, teachers and books, and professional skill which our towns and remote neighborhoods enjoy are the products of city institutions.

The influence of the city press alone, every week, is powerful beyond calculation upon millions of minds. The earliest news hastens to and from the city; the most startling and thrilling exhibitions of depravity are there reported. Thither the country looks for the most sagacious conjectures of what is to come. The city press is sometimes a combination of whatever is corrupt and debasing; but it is also often marked with whatever is quick, powerful and comprehensive in intellect, and almost as resistless as Fate. There is not such a newspaper reading population on the globe as that of America. The intelligence thus imparted and the sharpening of the faculties of our people by means of public lectures and schools, and the influence of the Sabbath with its schools, libraries, and pulpits, are all working out the great destiny of this nation. It is in such a great school-house, with the press and the temple of a pure Christianity for his instructors, that every American has his place from earliest youth even to the end of his days.

The influence of great cities, then, is the combined influence of *wealth and mind.* When a favored spot has been selected for the building of a city, men gather there; the laborer, the mechanic, and the merchant. These must have houses to dwell in, and they must have sustenance. This creates a market. Laborers, mechanics and merchants, are sometimes sick; this brings the physician; and sometimes they quarrel, this brings lawyers and justices and creates courts. Teachers, too, are needed to instruct their children, and ministers of the Gospel to remind them of a world to come. The wants of such a population bring ships with their cargoes, and the introduction of foreign products calls for home manufactures to pay for them, and this exchange of products introduces fashion, taste, rivalry, and skill, and activity in the pursuit of wealth. Great cities are thus the exchange places of commerce, agriculture, and manufactures, and these exchanges can not be made without leaving heavy deposits, and the richer and larger the surface of the world that trades to a particular city, the greater will be that city in wealth and population. Mental efforts are usually put forth either by high excitement or for large rewards of money. Both of these are found in cities. The city capitalist and merchant, are more likely to be men of strong intellect, than the nobleman that pretends to trace his blood back to William the Conqueror, or Charlemagne. No men need keener wits, or more mature judgments, and more accurate and extensive views, than the merchants of large cities. Large fortunes may be made or lost, as their knowledge of different countries and markets may be correct or imperfect. The web of social policy is never more intricate than when wrought from the threadwork of commerce. If I am not mistaken, no courts require more available intelligence on all subjects than the commercial. They are calculated to elicit a keen, a comprehensive, and a robust, if not a highly refined intelligence. The most flourishing schools of literature, and of the learned professions; the universities that mold the mind of the world, are found in Paris, Berlin, Rome, Leipsic, Edinburgh, and other large towns and cities in Europe and America.

The country and the village may be the best place for the birth and early training of youth; but it is in the excitement of the city that the highest developments of mind are made. The powerful minds that have swayed the destinies of mankind, though not commonly born in the great city, have generally gone to reside there, to feel the pressure of that activity which would draw out their strength, and to find a theater suitable for their talents. Our men of letters have their homes in or near our largest cities. Hume, whose authority is great in all matters of mere literary experience, says that "a great city is the only fit residence for a man of letters." This is true. In the country there may be leisure, but there will be a want of impulse for intellectual pursuits. The mind languishes in the midst of a wilderness. "'Tis better," in the development of intellect, "to dwell in the midst of alarms, than reign" in a horrible solitude. The mind without congenial spirits stagnates. "It gathers the rust of decay," as the immortal Chalmers says, "by its mere distance from sympathy and example." See his Polity of Cities. It is in the presence of libraries and of literary men, and under the pressure of intense excitement, that the human mind ordinarily comes forth in its greatest power. The leading men in all departments of city life are generally from the country; but it is *in* the city they encounter one another, and iron sharpeneth iron. Here they wrestle, they struggle, they grapple, they fall, they rise, and they run together—and, side by side, and urged on by the same kind of motives, they aim at the same goal. Here rivalry, excitement, and discussion evolve the highest kind of mental discipline, the keenest perception of things, and the loftiest sweep of intelligence and mental vision. Here the gravest questions on morals, politics, and religion, are agitated and discussed, decided upon, and settled. Here the highest kind of professional skill is called for, under the pressure of the most intense excitement, and the largest reward. In great cities have been made the decisions in law which have settled great national principles, and given stability to the whole of society; the discoveries in medicine which have alleviated the woes of countless myriads; the improvements in art, which have thrown the world forward, centuries at a single leap; and the investigations in science and learning, which have gradually changed the whole face of society. Where, but in a city, flowed forth the eloquence that "shook the arsenal, and fulmined over Greece to Macedon and Artaxerxes' throne?" In cities have been brought forth the wonderful creations of the pencil; poetry has tuned her loftiest rythm amid countless throngs of stirring men, and "the waters of Helicon" have gushed forth from paved streets and narrow lanes. Homer, Socrates, Shakspeare, Blackstone and Milton lived in cities. Socrates and the Son of Mary taught alike in the city and in the desert waste. The influence of Rome was so decided, that when it became Christian, the empire was converted, and when she fell under the weight of her corruption, the empire fell as if smitten with a palsy through every ligament and fiber. And all the world knows that Paris is France, and that, as that city decrees, the mighty French nation is a republic or a monarchy. And not only so, but as Paris dresses, so dresses the world. The caprice or taste of a Parisian, gives style to courts, and to all refined nations. Jerusalem was Judea, and with its subversion, the Jewish polity ceased. The cry of independence first raised in Mechlenberg county, North Carolina, was responded to by a mighty voice from Boston; and from the New England metropolis went forth the strong pulsations that severed the United Colonies from the British crown. The mighty heart of the British Empire is London, the greatest city of ancient or modern times. The government is there; the wealth is there; the press is there; the mind is there; the hilt of the sword is there. The whole world is under contribution by means of England's commerce supported by her navy, for its wealth, luxury, and glory. The whole world feels its every pulsation.

The thinkings of the British Cabinet run along the nerves of civilization, to the extremities of the globe. If such be the fearful influence of cities upon national destiny, it is a matter of infinite moment that they should be pervaded with sound principles. Our cities must be filled with the waters of life that the whole nation may drink and live. If they become the centers of pollution, their tainted streams will flow forth afar and in every direction; if, by means of corruption and vice, they become the great slaughter-houses of our young men, fearful will be the doom that will inevitably overtake the nation. But we read the future with hope and confidence. The hitherto almost impassable gulf that separated the ignorant from the educated is bridged. An aggressive movement of light is made upon the darkness that has hitherto covered the poor. Sympathy is beginning to pour a drop of comfort into the cup of filth and poverty. Now, the poor man sees the fair temple of science open to his children. The darkened mass is beginning to live. A hope of respectability and of rising from suffering to comfort and enjoyment is infused into the mass. The mind of the multitude is beginning to be enlightened and inspired with a taste for the beautiful and the good, and with a desire for cleanliness of person, of clothes, and habitation —with a taste for the morning paper, and for flowers, and for the charms of domestic bliss, there is hope for the purification of the heart. There is hope that order, and sobriety, and industry will supplant idleness, ignorance, and depravity. And as every human soul has a right patent from the Almighty for knowledge, so must the children of the street, and of the alley be gathered into our public and Sabbath-schools. The wealthy and the benevolent must strive together to improve, refine, and elevate the public taste by libraries, scientific lectures, and halls of painting and statuary. The million must be baptized into knowledge and charity. The poor man must be made to feel that respectability and comfort here, and life everlasting are indeed within his reach—that the promise of the Gospel, of a free education, and of unfettered political rights, as well as of his Maker's Bible and of his Maker's grace, is unto him and his children forever.

LECTURE II.

II.

TRADE AND LETTERS:

THEIR CONNECTION AND INFLUENCE ON THE PROGRESS OF NATIONS.*

Liberal trade is good scholarship popularized, and Commerce is literature on a sign-board.

A MERE tithe of reflection on the part of an audience so intelligent as the one I have to address, will show that great breadth of knowledge in our day attaches to the art of the farmer, and of the navigator, without whose joint labors mankind can neither be happy, nor progress as nations. Our banks, warehouses, express-offices, and custom-houses, and steamers, and clippers, are nothing without trade, and without them and the trade which is their life-blood, where were our halls of art and science, and asylums, and temples? If some brief and fragmentary thoughts on *Trade and Letters—their connection and influence on national progress*, are likely to be useful anywhere, I have ventured to hope they would be acceptable

* Delivered before the Mercantile Library Association, of San Francisco, in Musical Hall, on Tuesday evening, November 27th, 1855.

before so intelligent; energetic, and practical a body as the Mercantile Library Association of San Francisco, who are the pioneers and founders of a vast empire on the Pacific coast—whose influence is to travel with the orb of day and expand with his genial rays over the globe. Our position as an infant State, renders this subject an eminently practical one. Before it was known that there were mountains of gold in this State, it was said that the American's creed was utility—to do the most and get the most, in the shortest time. If this were so, then, without doubt his history now from the cradle to the grave is all in the imperative mood of the infinitive conjugation of the verb, to do—to do worship to the almighty dollar. At least, gentlemen, I conceive our times and responsibilities attach practical urgency to the consideration of such a subject. Whatever we do here, we do for coming ages, and what we fail to do, that we should do, is a fraud upon millions yet to be born.

I. The fifteenth and sixteenth centuries were the seed-sowing time of what Europe and America now are. Almost all the great events that now distinguish Christendom, may be traced up to those times. The present state of science and literature, of the ornamental and useful arts, of trade and social improvement, and of political knowledge and rights, may be traced back to the revival of letters, consequent upon, and connected with the discovery of America, the Reformation, commenced by Luther and his fellow-laborers, the invention of the art of Printing, and the discovery of the passage to India, by the Cape of Good Hope. In the progress of nations to wealth and power, various movements may be observed, and some of them may appear to be disconnected or antagonistic, but a more careful study of their respective histories reveals the fact, that their development has been through a graduated series, the one preparing for the other, and rising higher than the previous one; that sometimes the upward tendency has been checked, sometimes thrown back; but that on the whole there has ever been somewhere, a Goshen-spot, a rainbow-girt glen, where man has continued to struggle for progress in truth, and victory over the typhoon of evil, and where the light that was in him could not be crushed out, nor his hopes be driven to despair. In some spot or other of our globe, the sacred fire of liberty has always been kept burning, and in due time, the vestal flame will make luminous all the dark places of the earth. I am aware that there is a school of prophets who never see any thing hopeful in the horoscope of our race. I am not one of these. Thank God, I do not belong to that school. Over the field of carnage and death, I see the rainbow of promise. When I find the door of civilization rusted on its hinges in Asia, and fallen from its portals in Africa, and covered in ruins on the Acropolis, I remember the flight of "pious Æneas," bearing old Anchises; I remember that it has raised new temples in other hemispheres, and that here its doors are flung wide open, and by our Public Schools, the latch strings are hung on the outside, so that whosoever will, may come, and whosoever is athirst may enter and drink from the living fountains of knowledge.

From the day that the first man began his toiling pilgrimage, the earth has not lacked a civilized man to rule over it. The oldest monumental records of our race are records of man's highest civilization in "the gray dawn of time." The further back we go in Egypt's history, the higher are its forms of civilization; and it is now an admitted fact by the *savans* of Europe, that civilization entered Africa, by the isthmus of Suez, and then ascended the Nile. The colonies from the Euphrates began the mighty empire of the Nile by building a temple at Heliopolis for the worship of the setting sun.* There is a tendency in the waters on the African coast to flow westward; this creates the great equatorial current that breaks against South America, and expending some of its force by sending off branches north and south, flows on itself through the Caribbean sea; and here, growing warm, it flows through the Gulf of Mexico, as if trying to get

* See Osborne's 'Monumental Egypt," passim.

farther west; but being opposed by headlands, it is obliged to trace its way along the Atlantic side of this continent, to Newfoundland, and then shoots across the Atlantic to Europe; and as it goes, throws its lesser waves upon Iceland, and the Arctic sea.

And so great is the force of this equatorial current, heated in the passage of the Gulf of Mexico, that it actually changes the line of perpetual frost, and carries it several degrees further north. But for the warmth of the equatorial current thrown upon northern Europe, a very large portion of Russia, Norway, Sweden, and Lapland, would be perpetually frozen. Thus the fate of countries, and the lives of millions of men, are made to depend on a circumstance so slight as to be almost unknown or overlooked. If this great current could make its way through the Isthmus of Panama, or of Tehuantepec, to the Pacific, instead of being compelled to make its way north, what would happen? Why, if the Gulf Stream were poured into the Pacific, it would not raise the temperature of the higher latitudes of Europe, and, as a consequence, a large portion of those countries that are now the granaries of men and beasts, would become deserts of ice. It is owing to the heat diffused by the Gulf Stream, on its northward progress, that France and Great Britain are so much milder in winter than the same latitudes in America. Now, this rebounding of the currents that flow westward from the equatorial east, is a significant fact. If the waves of immigration have brought principles, institutions and races, from the East to our shores, it is that they may be quickened, warmed into a better, a higher life, as the equatorial current, and then made to flow back, to regenerate, beautify, enrich, and save the Old World. As a considerable portion of Europe would be frozen up but for the warmth of the return current from the New World—so would it have starved but for our wheat-fields; and would have sunken into the torpor of hopeless tyranny but for the impulses of Young America, whose example is galvanizing it into newness of life. But seriously, I apprehend there is the same natural tendency in the stream of civilization, that we find in the equatorial current. It began to flow in nearly the same direction, and has been arrested by the same continent, and is now rebounding in the same general course. And is not this a kind of prophetic omen to us, through the beneficence of Providence that is ever gracious to man, pointing out to this new world its high mission!

But geology, not less than geography, is our teacher and prompter. The geologist tells us that the crust of our globe consists of certain strata subsisting in certain well-defined relations to each other. That is, in regard to position, one stratum is higher than another. And that this position of the superponent masses is owing to the convulsions of the last days of the dynasty immediately preceding the advent of our race upon the planet, and that wherever we find these stratified rocks, the same relative position which they have in one part, will hold good all over the globe, unless where, from some extraordinary circumstance, this natural position has been disturbed. Just so is it with human races. By some terrible moral catastrophe, they are all found in the same stratified position, except where, by the agency of some great extraneous power, some of them have been raised above it. As man came from the hand of his Maker, he was highly civilized. But by a sad delinquency he lost his innocence. In him, however, were left the seeds or germs from which by great culture in coming ages, he might repair the ruins of his fall. And hence, human progress is widely different, at different times and among different races; but no instance has ever occurred of a savage nation raising itself to civilization, without aid from abroad. A foreign element has, in every instance, been introduced. And this element now is found to be Christianity. This as a mere reviewer of the world's progress, I am bound to say, and without affirming any thing as to its Divine origin. True or false, Christianity is now a world-wide fact, and the dominant influence in human history. To it the hopes of our race are turned, as the only light that can scatter the darkness that broods over the nations, and exorcise the unclean demons that have so long lorded it over the earth.*

II. The almost universal, and certainly the oldest traditions of the human race point to the interior of Asia as its cradle.† It is on the Mediterranean, the Persian Gulf, the Red Sea, and the Nile, that we find the oldest navigators mentioned in history, the Egyptians and Phenicians.‡ And to one of these very earliest of trading nations is said to belong the honor of inventing letters, if, indeed, they were invented, and to both the Egyptians and Phenicians, certainly, belongs the place in the world's history, of being the first and most devoted patrons of literature. They are not more famous for their commerce and building of cities than they are for their knowledge of letters. When they were the greatest traders and workers, and the most wealthy and powerful, then they were the most learned people in the world. Herodotus,§ the father of profane history, on many points is a doubtful authority, for he was, as most travelers are, the victim of his Phrygian dragoman. But beyond him, lies the unexplored territory of fable, conjecture, and uncertainty. Egypt's lying priests told him that the gods reigned over their country for eighteen thousand years before Menes, the

* See Appendix C. † See Appendix D.
‡ See Appendix E. § See Appendix F.

founder of their first mortal dynasty, but they throw not a ray of light on the world's early days. The same thing may be said of the Hindoo and Chinese records. They are not, after all, as old as Moses, and not to be believed, whether old or new. The Pentateuch is the oldest and only reliable record of what took place in the early ages of the world. It is only incidentally, however, that the inspired writers make mention of heathen nations.

As the original station allotted to man was in the East, so there our race began its career of travel and improvement. The wisdom of the East would therefore become proverbial at an early day, and its productions be in demand among the nations emerging from it. The remains of the sciences which were cultivated in India, as well as of the arts which were exercised there in remote ages, authorize us to conclude that it was one of the first countries in which man made any considerable progress.

ORIGIN OF TRADE.

Trade, doubtless, began with the awakening of human desire. I think the first bargain was made in Paradise, and it was a bargain to gratify the eye and taste, but it was a California bargain—a ruinous speculation. Cain, and Lamech, and Tubal-Cain, and the builders of cities, and the workers in metals, however, were not deterred from trading with Nimrod for skins and furs. The first trading after the flood was between the mothers and daughters of Noah's three sons, when they were packing up to come out of the ark, and no doubt it was then found that those who had been the neatest, and had preserved the best order in their part of the vessel, were able to make the best bargain, and I have but very little doubt that Shem's family were the best traders.*

For a considerable time the intercourse of the scattering families of these three great patriarchal fathers must have been carried on wholly by land and on foot. It was ordained, however, by the beneficent Creator, that man should have dominion over the beasts of the field. Accordingly, among his very first and most important conquests was that of the camel, without whose aid the vast deserts of Asia and Africa would be absolutely impassable. But as mankind became more and more numerous, and more widely dispersed, journeying between them became long, and toilsome, and perilous, and yet more and more frequent. It then happened that mercantile adventurers would collect together, and for mutual safety and comfort, form a temporary association, which was afterward called a caravan, and this was the original of our express, mercantile, and joint-stock companies.

Still, as emigration west and east, north and south pro-

* See Appendix G.

gressed, and the tribes of men became separated by rivers, and bays, and seas, it became more and more difficult to keep up trade and intercourse. Necessity then became the mother of invention, and rivers and arms of the sea, and the ocean itself was made man's carrier. Shipbuilding and navigation were a great advance upon foot carriers and camels. And from the raft or canoe that the savage constructed to ferry him over the river that he encountered in the chase, to the steamship of our day, the progress of improvement is immense. But when men were once able to travel by sea, trade soon took wings.

Ships are on water what rivers and railroads are on land. The earliest caravan routes, were along the rivers, and from one river to another. In early times, as now, rivers and mountains have much to do in shaping the course of the current of humanity, and in giving character to a country. Not only does a river have a great influence on the agricultural and manufacturing profits of a country, but on its products. Without the great rivers of this continent, its interior would be comparatively useless to our race. It would be less fertile, if not wholly barren, and its products much more expensive when delivered in the markets. Australia* is an example of what a continent may be without rivers. In many respects the Nile is one of the most wonderful rivers of our globe, and

* See Appendix H.

well illustrates the influence of a river in giving character to a country. For more than two thousand miles of wandering, it receives no tributary—not the smallest. And though its valley was called the granary of the Old World, and did actually sustain an immense population, and is still proverbial for its fertility; yet the Nile from its fountains to the sea flows through nothing but deserts. On the one side the Sahara stretches into the African continent for four or five thousand miles; and on the other, the Arabian and Asiatic, for some two thousand miles. All the countries bordering on the Nile are bounded by deserts, and but for it, they would themselves have formed a part of the great deserts of Arabia and Africa.

TRADE OF THE EAST ALWAYS DESIRED.

It is a singular fact, that ever since the dispersion of mankind from the valley of the Euphrates, when some came west, and some went east; those who came west have wanted the products that grew in the east; and that whatever nation has been the carrier of these products from the east to the west, has become rich and powerful; and that along whatever line this trade has vacillated, great cities have grown up; and when, and in the degree that that trade has been diverted, they have generally perished. For this, the Tyrians, Greeks,

Romans, Saracens, Venetians, Portuguese, Dutch, and English, are our monumental proof.

Alexander the Great penetrated to India by land, but found that the overland route thither by the Indus would not do. He therefore sent Nearchus with a fleet down the Indus to explore the Indian Ocean to the mouth of the Euphrates, but he was not satisfied with the valley of the Euphrates, and extended his idea of bringing the wealth of India to Europe by the way of the Red Sea and the Nile. He therefore fixed upon the western mouth of the river, as the place for a great city, and called it after himself, Alexandria. Nor was he mistaken. And as Alexandria grew by the Indian trade, so Petra, Palmyra, Tyre, and Constantinople, declined. Alexander's Syrian successors, and Antiochus the Great, Tamerlane, and Nadir Shah, all coveted the rich commodities of India, and the countries beyond. They led armies thither by land, or attempted to do so; but failed of their object. It is to Alexander the Great, more than any other man, Europe is indebted for the knowledge that a great city could be built up, and an empire erected by trading with the East. Alexander the Great* was the pioneer of the English East India Company.

Mohammed,† whether knave or fanatic, had the art of seeing what would enhance the power of his followers.

* See Appendix I. † See Appendix J.

In his injunction upon them, to visit once in their lifetime the *Caaba*, or square building, in the temple of Mecca, it is difficult to determine whether he did more to awaken and concentrate their religious feelings, or to awaken and extend their commercial desires.

As the Mohammedan religion spread with amazing rapidity over all Asia and a large part of Africa, and as its adherents were taught to make a pilgrimage to Mecca, so trade grew with the extension of their creed. Commercial intercourse by sea and land received a new impulse. From the shores of the Atlantic, and from the distant regions of the East, annually, large caravans of pilgrims wended their way to Mecca. Commercial ventures were mingled with devotion. Numerous camels had to be sold and bought. Large supplies for long journeys had to be provided. This bartering and selling, even for a holy pilgrimage, quickened their wits, increased their knowledge of the commodities produced in different countries, and readily suggested that a few camels might be loaded on speculation; and their utmost ingenuity would at the same time be exerted to find out the easiest mode of conveyance, the shortest route, the safest way, and the largest sale. The Koran had expressly taught them that they might trade during their pilgrimage to Mecca: "It shall be no crime in you, if ye seek an increase from your Lord, by trading during the pilgrimage." (Koran, ch. ii., p. 36.)

Accordingly the holy city became a mart for commerce. Here were the chintzes and muslins of Bengal and the Deccan, the shawls of Cashmere, and pepper and spice of Malabar, the diamonds of Golconda, the pearls of Kilcare, the cinnamon of Ceylon, the nutmegs, cloves, and mace, of the Moluccas, the silks of Persia and China, and an immense quantity of other oriental commodities. For a number of years, the mercantile transactions of the annual fair of Mecca, were the largest in the world. There was to be found whatever was deemed necessary for the preservation, and comfort of life, and for its elegance, and pleasure, and the costly things required for worship, and for the embalming of the body. Something to suit the taste of every climate, and the fancy of every superstition—for the "infidel" European, the luxurious Asiatic, and the rude natives of Africa.

In early times the Arabs were satisfied with national independence, and personal liberty. They tended their camels or reared their palm-trees within their own peninsular domain, and sought no further intercourse with the rest of mankind, than to sally out occasionally, and plunder a caravan, or rob a traveler. But their conquest of Egypt changed their habits, particularly as to trade, and their intercourse with other nations. It was to gain and hold a monopoly of trade, that Caliph Omar built Bassora. Nor was it long till they were the sole carriers between China and Europe. They pushed their discoveries further in the East, than had ever been done before, and from being the despisers of commerce, civilization and letters, they became their zealous promoters, and did actually make a considerable atonement for the burning of the Alexandrian Library, by their contributions to art, science, and literature. Their trade covered the Indian Archipelago. From the Red sea and Persian Gulf, their vessels plied to all the seas and harbors of China. Many Mohammedans settled in India, and in the countries beyond. Many of the inhabitants of India are Mohammedans to this day. Indeed, I believe her majesty, the Queen of Great Britain, has more Mohammedans in her dominions than the Sultan of the Ottoman Empire. So numerous were the Saracens, at one time, in Canton, that the Emperor allowed them a Cadi of their own religion. And the Arabian language was then in the East as the lingua Franca is now in the Levant. It was spoken in almost every known sea-port. To the Arabs Europe is indebted for the first reliable account of the tea-tree, and of the city of Canton, and of the Chinese manufacture of porcelain, as well as for the use of coffee.

When the Mohammedans became lords of Egypt, they would not allow Christians to trade through their empire to the East. Hence, they were compelled to seek out a way beyond the limits of the Saracen empire. Trade then flowed from north-western China and India, to Constantinople, by an interior land and sea route, requiring a journey of two hundred and fifty to three hundred days for camels. But from this trade Constantinople immediately received new life. The way, however, was long, and perilous. The caravans usually stopped on the Oxus, and their goods were carried down that river to the Caspian sea, up the river Cyrus, and then again by land over the portage to the Phasis, which flows into the Black sea, and thence by vessels to Constantinople. So much, however, did the trade with India and China increase the wealth and splendor of this city, that Robertson, the historian, boldly asserts that it retarded for some time the decline of the whole Roman empire, of which it was then the capital.

When the trade of India was carried, by the way of the Euphrates and the great Syrian Desert, to the Mediterranean, then arose "Tadmor in the Wilderness." It was the trade from the Persian Gulf with the West that raised Palmyra to great opulence and power. Its situation amid a few palm-trees, in the heart of the Desert, was unique. Its form of government, however, was republican, which, according even to Robertson, "is the best suited to the genius of a commercial city." With no other source of power and aggrandizement than the profits of the trade between the Euphrates and the Mediterranean, it grew in the heart of the Desert, to most astonishing wealth. Amid powerful and ambitious neighbors, it long maintained its splendor, and even rivaled Rome itself. Egypt, Syria, Mesopotamia, and a large portion of Asia Minor, were conquered by its arms, and its Queen, Zenobia, contested dominion with one of the most warlike Roman Emperors.

When the trade of the East changed from the Persian to the Arabian Gulf, then Babylon, Bassora, Palmyra, and Tyre declined, and Petra became the storehouse of Europe, and subsequently Alexandria, and those cities respectively, on the western side of the Mediterranean, which became its distributors of oriental merchandise. I have not time now to show why the West has always coveted the treasures of the East; nor why it is that oriental commodities are different from those of the West. But it is doubtless a wise and beneficent Providence. As the saltness, and eternal heaving of the ocean are ordained for good, so are the respective products of the different parts of the globe adjusted in such a way as to call forth effort and intercourse among men. There is doubtless the same philosophical necessity, and kind design, in the relative condition of the different parts of our globe, and its diversified products, that there is in the mutual attractions of the sexes. Whatever may be the philosophy of the matter, the fact is plain enough. So important has the trade of the East been deemed in all ages, both ancient and modern, that every nation and city, of any life, or lofty aspirations, has struggled to obtain it, and whatever city or nation has monopolized it, has thereby grown rich, and predominant in influence. In proof of this, you need only turn to the history of Tyre, Palmyra, Babylon, Petra, Byzantium, and Alexandria; and of Venice, "the bride of the sea;" of Genoa, "the superb, the city of places;" of Florence, the home of the arts; and of her daughter Bruges, the great store-house of her merchants for Europe, under the Hanseatic league, of Antwerp, Lisbon, and London. And in all these cases, not equally, but in all, prominently does it appear, that, as the oriental trade has enriched European cities, so have they become the homes of manufactures and the patrons of learning and science.

The discovery of a way to India by the Cape of Good Hope by Vasco de Gama, led to great revolutions, not only in the course of commerce, but also in the political state of Europe. Portugal pushed her trade at once into the East with such energy and judgment that she soon built up a commercial empire to which, for splendor and opulence, and also for the genius by which it was governed, other nations could offer no parallel.

We may form some idea also of the profits of the trade

carried on by the Venetians, previous to the discoveries of De Gama, with the East, from the interest they paid on money. By a treaty with Sultan Mahmoud, they monopolized the trade of Alexandria with Europe, and so profitable was this trade, that they could pay 20 per cent premium for money, and sometimes even a higher rate. The premium paid for the use of money is, perhaps, the best standard by which to measure the profits arising from the capital stock employed in commerce. During this time of high interest, the wealth of Venice, individual and public, increased almost beyond description or belief. The magnificence of the houses of her merchants, and the richness of their furniture, and the profusion of their plate, and their revenues were greater than those of the reigning princes of most other countries.

Two great events, however, caused the glory to depart forever from Venice, which she could neither have foreseen nor have prevented. These events have been already named—the passage to India by the Cape of Good Hope, and the discovery of America. The seats of power and wealth were now changed. Portugal and Spain rose to wealth, but Spain did not become commercial or literary, and consequently her wealth was neither abiding nor beneficial. The immense treasures of the New World were poured into her lap, but it was merely to be consumed. It was not employed in productive industry, nor distributed by trade, nor devoted by the promotion of science and general intelligence. She built some cathedrals, and palaces, and gilded domes; but, with immense wealth and domains, she sank into commercial torpor, ignorance, and poverty: and, like Venice, she leaves scarcely an honorable name to posterity, as the child of her glory in the New World.

Productive industry is essential to the permanent prosperity of a country. The Holland of to-day is not the Holland of the sixteenth and seventeenth centuries. What is there now to be seen in the almost deserted streets of Delft, Leyden, and Haarlem, but the sweet, hopeful faces of the Dutch women, who seem to be waiting, like the women at the sepulcher, for the return of the glory of the Low Countries. "The grass now grows through the seams of the brick pavements, and ragged clothes flutter in the wind, out of the drawing-room casements of the palaces; and the echo of wooden shoes, clattering through empty saloons, tells of past magnificence and present indigence." Why are the streets of Holland's cities silent, and her canals green with undisturbed slime? Because her commercial prosperity was not supported by productive industry. Her capital was not employed in producing what man consumes. She had scholars, theologians, and artists. Her literature grew with her commerce; but her genius and wealth were not so employed as to multiply her thinkers and workers, and keep command of the markets of the world. Her fields and shops did not keep pace with her ships and counting-rooms. She had no public schools nor mercantile libraries. She was a mere broker for other countries; and, as soon as they could become their own brokers, she was left behind in the race, and has finally buried herself within her own dykes; a plain proof that national greatness always implies progress. As soon as a nation ceases to grow, it begins to decay. Venice, Holland, and Spain are a demonstration that the greatness of a nation depends not on the amount of its wealth, but on the employment and distribution of its wealth, and its power to create wealth. This implies intelligence, industry, and integrity. A people pre-eminent in agricultural skill, and in manufacturing and in mining skill, are prepared to sustain vast commercial enterprises. The riches and glory of the world lie at their feet. The productions of all climes are at their command. The means of enjoyment and of advancement are in their hands.

IV. FINE ARTS AND USEFUL ARTS.

We have some knowledge of cities and empires partly commercial and partly military—of commercial greatness and military renown—that have perished. It remains for us to combine these with popular intelligence and a high moral culture, and by productive industry make our material prosperity progressive and abiding. In pleading for the highest mental culture, I do not sympathize with the reproaches that are cast upon us as a cold, machine-calculating, utilitarian people. After all, what does this cloud-rocked, dreamy love of the fine arts, in contradistinction to the useful arts, do for the improvement of our race? In developing the mental powers and moral qualities of human nature, they are not equal to works of benevolence, nor to the common useful arts. I have yet to learn that the painter, the sculptor, the musician, or the theatrical performer, is really a more cultivated, more intellectual, more refined and benevolent, or more moral member of society than the manufacturer, the mechanician, the engineer, the shopkeeper, or the merchant. I have yet to learn that the city of Rome, the mother of the fine arts, possesses a higher grade of morals, of intellect and piety, than Manchester or Boston. The fact is, lest we should be called New Zealanders or Digger Indians, or what is worse, unmannerly clowns, and be excommunicated from the pale of fashion, we are wont to attach an undue importance to the fine arts of the white kid tribe. I do not consider a picture, a statue, or a palace, so high an effort of human faculties, as a foundery, a printing-press, a cotton-mill, or a ship. Homer, Virgil, Dante, Milton, Shakspeare, Phidias, Praxiteles, Raphael, Michael

Angelo, Canova, were great, sublimely great, immortal men; but greater still are the scientific inventors and producers in the useful arts. The inventors of the spade, the shovel, and the hoe, of movable types, ship-masts and tiller-ropes, power-presses and telegraph wires, have wielded a greater influence for good than all the royal heads that have ever lived. They have opened up the earth and called forth its treasures for man's good. The exponent of the civilization and intellectual progress of our race now is not a statue, but a steam-engine—not an epic, but a telegraph. The toiling teacher who awakens thought and belabors a single mind into a consciousness of mental power, does more good than all the lisping amateurs that could hop and bow about in a saloon as long as from the Golden Gate to John O'Groat's house. The hard-handed manufacturer, who makes a printed cotton handkerchief, and the tarry-fingered sailor who carries that handkerchief to Africa, to adorn the woolly head of the ebony-faced daughters of the Mountains of the Moon, have done more for civilization and the extension of humanizing influences, than all the poets and professors of dillettanteism in the world.

I would seek for the general elevation of all classes of society, of the farmer and the mechanic, of the trader and merchant, as well as of the learned professions—because in our age all have peculiar opportunities for mental and moral improvement, and great moral responsibility rests upon all. History shows that as a people improve in knowledge, so their wants will increase, and the deeper will be their sensibility to their wants, and consequently, if they have the means of gratifying them, the more they will advance in civilization. It is plain, therefore, that the increase of luxuries may be made a blessing, and not a curse. And of all people in the world, it is the most important that Americans should know how to possess themselves of the power to pass hours of leisure either in solitary meditation, or of social discussion on the origin and nature of the human mind, and on the high duties of free and enlightened citizenship.

To govern others, we must first govern ourselves, and be established in virtuous habits, and our understanding enlightened with that knowledge which will enable us clearly to discern why we are called into existence, and also as to what is due from us to others, and to our Creator as well as to ourselves.

V. PROVIDENCE DESIGNS THE PROGRESS OF THE NATIONS.*

It is a singular Providence, that the discovery of America and of the passage to India by the Cape of Good Hope, should have occurred so nearly at the same

* See Appendix K.

time. In all ages the commodities of the East have been purchased with the precious metals. As the demand for oriental commodities was increased in Europe, by the opening up of the route thither by the Cape, so it was necessary that the supply of gold and silver should be increased. It was therefore just at the time that Europe was drained, that America opened her mines, and poured her treasure into the lap of the old world, far beyond what had ever before been known. And from that day to this the productions of India and China, if we except the "damning trade" in opium, have been purchased chiefly with the silver of Peru and Mexico. Nor is this the only way in which the new world has supplied the exhausted stores of the old. Her granary has poured forth bread to her millions, and furnished the raw material that has clothed and fed millions more, and but for the gold of California, the great nations now at war, would have been unable to set their squadrons in the field, or man their fleets before Sebastopol, or Cronstadt.

I am well aware that the connection I advocate between Trade and Letters, and their joint and reciprocal influence on the progress of nations, is in whole, or in part denied. But I submit candidly and confidently that the true reading of history makes it "palpable to the thinking," that with a revival of the commercial spirit of Europe, we had a revival of Letters, and a grand epoch in the progress of nations. The same thing is seen in ancient as well as in modern times. In the eighteenth dynasty of Egypt, her Augustan age, that kingdom was greatly in advance of the rest of mankind in the knowledge of agriculture as an art, and in the extent of her foreign commerce. And in all that remains of that dynasty, we have evidences of a high state of the arts, of skill and labor, and of extended trade, and as a consequence its monumental history tells us that during that dynasty there was a great increase both of public and private wealth by foreign trade.* The very same thing is true of the Hebrew monarchy under Solomon. His ships were the world's carriers. Its gold therefore filled his capital. His kingdom was more extensive than the Hebrew dominions had ever been before, or than they ever were afterward. But who of all Israel's kings was an author and patron of Letters, like the royal preacher, the son of David? Is it not by her commercial genius that Europe discerns the respective wants and resources of all the other great nations of the earth, and by rendering them reciprocally subservient to one another, has gained a tremendous power over them, and derived from them an immense increase of opulence, power, and elegant enjoyment? It is also a notable fact that the promoting causes of the progress of nations, the moral and physical improvements of society,

* See Osborne's "Monumental History of Egypt," vol. i., 376, 377.

have not had their rise among hierarchies, aristocracies and the proprietors of entailed landed estates. Too often have the exploits of conquerors who have desolated the earth, and the freaks of tyrants who have slaughtered whole nations, been recorded with a disgusting accuracy, and fulsome adulation, while the discovery of useful arts, and the progress of the most beneficial branches of trade, have been passed over in silence, and suffered to sink into oblivion. The great moral and physical improvements of society have usually begun with practical, hard-working men, who have most keenly felt their necessity. Almost all improvements in conducting business, inventions, and discoveries, have had their origin among a hard-working and trading people. It is the mercantile class and the active and industrious mechanic that tread on the heels of what has already been achieved, and therefore feel the necessity of doing something by which they can advance. When the analysis of soils, or the invention of machinery, or the deep thinking and profound experimentings of the laboratory have brought to light something that can be turned to the use of the laborer, it is the trading town that fosters it and pays for it. Every extension of commerce is like opening a new avenue for blessings upon society. As commerce is enlarged, so is labor divided, and the demand for money, and exchange, and handicraft of every kind, increased.*

* See Appendix L.

And the very magnitude of the commercial transactions of our day, enhances the obligation to high morality in trade. An enlargement of commerce carries with it an augmented necessity for punctuality and integrity. If integrity is not the rule of a trade that encircles the globe, and is spoken in a hundred tongues, exposure, decline, and ruin are certain consequences. The more money we have, and the more extended our credit and trade, the greater is the necessity for rigid business morality. And in spite of the forgeries and frauds that disgrace our age from Australia and California to New York, London, and Paris, I dare affirm, and that without eulogizing the piety of our merchant princes, that modern trade gains every year in the standard of a high morality. The appearance to the contrary lies on the surface, and is chiefly among officials rather than in legitimate trade, and appears greater than it really is by comparison, because the comparison is made with commercial transactions much more extended both as to their territory and their intrinsic amounts—and also because wherever the English tongue is their vehicle, there great publicity is given to every instance of bad faith, or of dishonesty. It is absolutely certain that trade can not thrive or be a permanent blessing without a rigid morality. As religion is contaminated by hypocrites, as statesmanship is brought into discredit by noisy politicians, so is trade degraded by rogues. But its legitimate tendency is to enlarge the mind, and to produce punctuality and honesty. Dishonest traders are false to their calling.

VI. LABOR-SAVING MACHINERY.

Smith and McCulloch, great names on such a subject, tell us that the saving of labor and time by machinery, and by a division of labor, adds to national wealth, for it enables the laborer to employ his time and strength in other employments, or to devote himself to such practice and pursuits as may enable him to reach higher perfection in his chosen art or trade. All that is wanted, then, is room and means, for all to find productive employment, and then, the more laborers, and the more labor by machinery, the greater will be the product of our industry, and consequently, the greater will be the strength of the country. Every pound of steam employed in pumping water out of the mines, or in moving machinery, or in grinding grain or quartz, adds to our national wealth, because the men that would be employed in pumping out the water, or in grinding by hand engines, or implements in their own unaided strength, can be occupied with other productive labors. If there were not room for all who want employment—if there were not millions of acres that want hands—her labor-saving machinery might interfere with the profits of the poor man's toil. But while the door is open, as with us, and motives are presented for more and higher inventions, and increased labor, there is not wanting any thing needful to call forth our energies. We have capital, commerce, and foreign markets, we have rich lands, mines of coal, lead, silver and gold. We have every thing to produce a national pre-eminence, such as the world has never known, if we are faithful to the behests of Providence.

VII. DOMESTIC AND FOREIGN TRADE.

Without the activity, physical and mental, produced by, and necessary to, the carrying on of extensive domestic and foreign trade, *popular intelligence would be a thing unknown.* The great advantage of trade to a city and a State consists in this: it pushes the division of labor to the furthest extent, and brings its population under the strongest motives to exertion, and supplies them with many necessaries and comforts of life, which, by their own individual efforts, they could not procure. As commerce is not a direct but an indirect source of wealth, it must be both domestic and foreign. The capital of a nation must be employed in productive industry within itself, as well as in sending out ships to other lands. McCulloch declares, there is "no reason for thinking that we should have been at this day advanced beyond the point to which our ancestors had attained during the Heptarchy, had Great Britain been cut off from all intercourse with strangers. It is to the products and the arts derived from others, and to the emulation inspired by their competition and example, that we are mainly indebted for the extraordinary progress we have already made, as well as for that we are yet destined to make."

There are rural districts in Europe and in our transmontane States, where the father of a family lives and dies as if tethered to the column of his own chimney's smoke, unable to give the traveler the necessary directions to find his way to the neighboring village, whose church steeple has glittered in the sunshine before him all his life time. But it is not so in the trading village. The shrill morning cry of the newsboy with red nose and ragged elbow is a potent call to thought, to inquiry, and to reflections that lead to knowledge. In a traveling and trading community without formal text books and set hours in study, there is a sharp process of education going on all the time. Knowledge like sparks from a flint is flying about. And here and there, the sparks will catch, and acuteness, and expansion, and power of mind will appear. Without intercourse between different communities there is but little variety of occupation. A dull monotony like a nightmare lies upon the character. It is when trade opens up a market for the products of the milk of the dairy, the shop and the poultry-yard, that there is an awakening and a competition. And out of this ambition of style, of fashion, and feeling of rivalry, something good may come. It is as men have settled dwelling-places, and begin to adorn their homes, that they will begin to think of books and pictures, and indulge in intellectual pleasures. And as is the demand so will the supply be. Accordingly the literature of commercial nations is not composed chiefly of such materials as entered into the prevailing literature of the age of Pericles, of Augustus, or of Louis XIV. The literature that prevails in any community acts upon it, and then is itself affected. The patronage it receives is the air upon which it lives. It is a reflection of the public taste. It is a Texas tree-frog, that is black or green according to the prevailing color of the branches where it finds lodging. And hence the style and form of literature are subject to changes like the furniture of a drawing-room, or the contents of a wardrobe. Again, apart from the INCENTIVES of trade, the higher developments of intellect in relation to science would never have been made. Mental capacities of the highest order are required for the management of commercial affairs. The making or the losing of large fortunes sometimes depends upon the information that comprises a knowledge of markets and supplies all over the globe. The result of an operation depending of course upon the information as to its being correct and timely, or incorrect, or too late. And hence it is that few statesmen have been superior to those that have grown up in the midst of great commercial cities, or have represented great mercantile interests*—the great mass of those engaged in trade, and even of those who in trading communities are citizens of the world. And as their knowledge of mankind is extended by mingling in the great world around them, so their prejudices are modified. And the consciousness that they are citizens of the great world, combined with the power that wealth gives, makes their homes the centers, where nearly all the civil liberty of mankind has been preserved, and from which it has been diffused among the nations. It is said that the absorption of the mind of a shop-keeping and trading people is so great, that they are incapable of appreciating the beauty of Letters—that the highest culture can only be reached by men of a higher order of genius and more devoted to the pursuit of knowledge, than belongs to the producers, carriers, and brokers of mankind. But I apprehend it requires no argument to prove that a taste for literature and the refinements of good society may be attained without matriculation into College Halls. It may be created and elevated by the means and embel-

* See Appendix M.

lishments of life procured through trade and by intercourse with the world. What is called a liberal education is greatly to be desired. Colleges and Universities are essential to the development of a nation's strength. But if the encouragement of the fine arts in Europe and America had been left wholly to noble blood and that order of genius that can alone fully appreciate works of art, and the higher pursuits of literature, then our race had been deprived of nine tenths of all that is now our boast.*

VIII. CONNECTION OF TRADE AND LETTERS.

There are honored names, and not a few, that might be given in proof of the connection that may, and ought to exist between trade and letters, and of the progress of nations in benevolence and science, as they have increased in wealth and power. The wealthiest men of Europe in their day, were Cosmo and Lorenzo de Medici.† And yet they were merchants, farmers, bankers, and miners, and more pre-eminent still for their generosity and devotion to letters. To this family belongs the honor of having restored the empire of science and true taste to Europe after a dreary night of darkness. By their efforts many valuable manuscripts were saved from total destruc-

* See Appendix N. † See Appendix O.

tion. The Medici thought the discovery of a manuscript equivalent to the conquest of a kingdom. It is doubtful if we are not indebted to them for most of the perfect copies now known of the Greek and Roman classics. It is remarkable too, that Providence should have raised up these men to find and preserve so many valuable manuscripts just before the invention of printing, and just before the wonderful extension of discoveries and trade. The Medici were educated as merchants, and yet devoted their energies for a long life time to collect manuscripts, and found libraries, and extend their commercial relations. In the period of thirty years, they are known to have expended in relieving the poor, nearly seven hundred thousand florins. Their wealth followed chiefly from their monopoly of the trade of the East, but amid all the care and complications of increasing commercial relations, and of making improvements in manufacturing, and on their Italian farms and vines, they never seemed to lose sight of man's true dignity; nor of the proper objects of his regard. The same re-union of a commercial spirit with generosity, and the promotion of popular education is seen in the United States and Great Britain. Who but merchants enabled Lady Franklin to continue her long search for a lost but gallant husband? And who but a merchant and a banker (Grinnell and Peabody) have sent out the exploring expedition under the heroic Kane?

Again, as trading towns and cities are but storehouses of commerce, we are justified in considering their relation to science and education as a proof of the connection which exists between trade and letters. I speak not now of the materials—the facts and discoveries that trade has contributed to science and literature, but of the fact, that commercial and scientific knowledge are interwoven in the texture of all cities. Without the mental activity natural to men associated together, there would have been but little, if any progress in any department of human knowledge, and consequently no advance in civil rights. In the monumental fragments of the great cities of other days we are able to trace their developments of thought, reasoning, imagination and taste. It may be that the patronage of letters and science by trade and wealth is, in some measure, mercenary and vain. There is, indeed, something of vanity and selfishness in all human enterprises; but the encouragement to art and science is none the less real. It is of but little moment to our Powers, whether the order inclosing five thousand dollars for a bust flows from domestic affection, from patriotic fervor, or from vanity or pedantry. It is enough for the toiling chemist, artist, teacher, or author, that his works are appreciated at least so far as to get abroad in the world, and procure bread for him and his, and a fair opportunity for him to work out his mission. We can not always be worshiping the beautiful in the gilded, sequestered Madeleine of our imagination. We have to do with stern realities, that require the useful as well as the beautiful. We must draw inspiration then from Arkwright, Watt, Fulton, and Davy, as well as from Canova, Milton, Aristotle, and the *divine* Plato.

The investigation of this subject has impressed upon my mind some remarks which I have seen in the newspapers about New York and Canton. The contrast is a striking illustration of the influence of Christian Letters on national well-being. The contrast is to the following effect. New York and Canton are about the same size as to population. The one is the great commercial emporium of the East, as the other is of the West. They are on nearly opposite sides of the planet. One particular is selected as an exponent of the known and unknown well being of humanity in the two cities. In Canton while they were chopping off heads at the rate of about eight hundred per day, until some seventy thousand victims were executed, many of whom were skinned alive and then hacked to pieces at the leisure or pleasure of the executioners, on the other hand in the western emporium, the same mail that brought us the news of the Canton executions, informed us that the New Yorkers were looking at the happy faces and listening to the simple songs of three thousand children, whom misfortune had placed in need of their kindness. Now why this difference? Canton is ten times older than New York, and should, therefore, be ten times wiser? In manufacturing industry, too, Canton is in advance of her western rival. Fifty thousand persons are said to be employed in manufacturing cloth in Canton, and nearly twenty thousand in silk weaving, and the workers in wood, stone, iron, brass, and leather, beyond computation. Nor is Canton poor in literature, such as it is. She has fourteen high schools, and about thirty colleges. Her commerce is large, but she herself is a mere dépôt or storehouse. The ships that trade with her are not hers, nor do they belong to her side of the world. They rest at her wharves as mere birds of passage. The root of the difference then between these cities lies in the difference there is between a false and a true religion. Canton has one hundred and twenty *temples*, while New York has one hundred and sixty *Christian Churches*. The temples of Canton are dedicated to a horrid superstition, the essence of which is hate and malignity. The religion taught in them is false and is embodied in false theories of the earth, and identified with false science, and in every way an obstacle to the awakening of the mind, and its emancipation from error, and opposed to the enlargement of trade and the extension of fraternal intercourse among mankind. Among the Chinese there is no creative genius, no originating mind—no invention. They are mere imitators. Their being is the monotony of the tread-mill. There is no life, no expansion, no upward tendency. A false religion mildews their manufacturing, commerce, and letters. But the churches of New York are dedicated to the one living and true God. The essence of the religion taught in them, is peace on earth and good will to men. Expansion, benevolence, piety: these are its attributes. Its advance is marked by discoveries, inventions, and the outgoings of trade. It fosters science, and the fine and useful arts. The influence of religion on mankind is itself a theme deserving far more attention than it has received. The influence is seen in the deep and all pervading traditions of all nations—the strong hold it has on their hopes and fears—and in the many colonies that have been planted from religious motives. Its sanctuaries have become dépôts of trade as well as the radiating points of light. And not a few articles of trade have become such in order to supply the wants of the devotee. Scarcely one among all the half civilized nations of the ancient world would dare offer a gift to their gods without the frankincense or aromatic perfumes of Arabia. It is also well known that modern missions have been important auxiliaries to the extension of science and trade. The most important element in modern civilization is Christianity. We are painfully conscious that our cities are not the homes of saints, but the worst form of true religion is immeasurably better than the best form of a radically false one. Sadly imperfect as the Christianity of the commercial emporium of our Republic may be, it is immeasurably superior to the system of faith and morals that prevails in the Buddhist emporium on the other side of our globe.

It is true that natural science has a direct and powerful money bearing on the property of men, and that moral science has an equally direct and powerful bearing on their happiness. Without a knowledge of the natural capabilities of a country, and of their relations to the comfort and welfare of man, its inhabitants will remain ignorant and weak. And without letters, or a written literature, no nation has ever made great progress in knowledge or art. It is the light of science that teaches us how to multiply one acre so as to make four of it. That is, so to improve its cultivation as to make it yield as much as four would produce without such improvements, and then to make its yield effective in like proportion. The light of experience under the tutorship of science makes one ship now as valuable as a whole fleet was a few centuries ago. In increasing the *quantity* of our agricultural and manufacturing products, the light of experience and science also improves their *quality*, and increases their demand, and the facilities of trade for supplying that demand. It is by improvements in agriculture and in the art of navigation that countries comparatively sterile and far removed from markets are able to enter into successful competition with richer soils and more favored localities. But the knowledge of these improvements is not born with us, nor can we acquire it by yawning, nor by mere absorption as an oyster obtains his subsistence. Effort is the price that must be paid for the experience and science that make the arts of peace so poweful. Hence we want public schools, high schools, colleges, lyceums, galleries of the fine arts, scientific lectures, and the aid of the printing press, and the countenance and support of all classes to such enterprises as foster the growth of knowledge and elevate public sentiment. Though the fine arts and literature have in all ages been found in close connection with human progress, it is in comparatively modern times only that institutions have been established with an avowed or sole reference to the improvement of the mercantile classes.

Finally. I hope I have succeeded in showing that the new ideas of the value and importance of commerce and the new channels of trade made known to Europe by the discovery of America and of the passage of the Cape of Good Hope, mark the line of the chief distinction between the manners and political institutions of modern and ancient times. I hope enough has been said to show,

I. That the progress of a nation is just in the ratio of its skill in the employment of capital in productive industry, and in commercial enterprises.

II. That foreign as well as domestic trade sustained by the employment and distribution of wealth in productive industry is as necessary to the healthful progress of nations, as the circulation of the blood and the inhaling of fresh air is to the health of the body. And,

III. That such a progress requires the harmonious working of capital, and skill in all the industrial, useful, and ornamental arts that have distinguished the greatest nations of past ages.

IV. That trade and intercourse with mankind is necessary to the development of the individual species, and of national resources. The nations of the West have been a traveling, trading, noise-making, fighting, and at times a blustering family. But with them travels the power of the race. The Japanese, Chinese, and Hindoos, are a fair sample of what nations are, even with a high home-made literature, shut out from intercourse with the great world. The children of the East, according to their tribes, have vailed their women, and palissaded themselves with castes, or surrounded themselves with walls and refused to trade with the rest of mankind. And what is the result?

Degeneracy of every kind covers their whole escutcheon. As goods in bales unopened to the sun spoil; as plants in cellars without light and air languish; so are individuals and nations without intercourse with their fellow-men. It is a knowledge of what our neighbor has done or can do, that teaches us what we can do. It is a part of the Divine allotment that men should divide the earth among themselves, and jostle and elbow one another through it, in order to keep the weeds down, and the wild beasts in subjection. Commerce is the salt that preserves the ocean of life. But for trade and the literature necessary to carry it on, one half of the globe would now be covered with jungle, chapparel, and cactuses, and the other half inhabited by such smoke-dried specimens of humanity as the Camanches and our brethren of the "Flowery Kingdom."

As the European and civilized American nations require the commodities of the East, as the nations that are the carriers of these commodities command the most powerful resources of wealth and influence, so are we literally and actually, geographically and commercially, in the PATHWAY OF EMPIRE. The wealth of the world, and the hopes of future generations are before us. In doing our duty is our glory. And as with us rests especially the privilege of "rounding chaos into form," on this vast coast, so the responsibility devolving upon us as patriots and philanthropists is of fearful magnitude. This must be felt by every one who may consider the influence of this coast fifty years hence. As the pioneer population of the older States are here arrested by a flood of waters they can neither swim nor bridge, so will they beat back and fill up the mountains and the valleys of this continent until they shall beam with life and riches subservient to human comfort and elegance, as a beehive on the western prairies does with honey-making citizens. These radiant shores are destined to reflect a tremendous influence upon the great valley of the Mississippi by way of the Cordilleras and Rocky Mountains, and thence to the St. Lawrence and to Europe. I speak not now of the influence of California upon the ship-building and the looms of the Atlantic States, nor of her gold in Wall-street, Lombard-street, and the Bourse. Nor do I speak altogether of reflective influences. For the day will come, sure as the ordinances of heaven, when our Pacific States shall rival the Atlantic. We look out upon the richest portions of the earth, and upon the broadest ocean of our planet. The commerce of the East, the desire of all great nations, on its way to Europe, is coming to us. Nor is there a sheet now catching the wide ocean breeze, that does not carry the influence of California in its folds. Nor is there an invoice registered, or a bill of exchange drawn, that is not affected by the auriferous dust under our feet. It is then for the Eu-

REKA State, by her popular intelligence and public morality, and geographical and commercial position and relations, to mold the political and moral future of the entire Pacific world, from Panama to Cape Horn and Behring's Straits, and from the icy ocean to Jerusalem. The race of people now here, their antecedents, institutions, language, religion, and present position, and acknowledged aspirations, clearly foretell that in sober verity, their "manifest destiny" is to advance. The continent, the boundless continent, is theirs. Their order of mind, as well as their form of civilization, renders them the most powerful and fit people on earth to impress their character upon their neighbors. The English language is gradually, but certainly making itself the channel of communication in every sea-port, and along every coast of the world. No other language is spreading like it. It is in this tongue LIGHT from this coast will, at no very distant day, pencil into living pictures of beauty the thousand islands that repose on this vast ocean, and make luminious the mountains and harbors of Japan and China, and travel up the Amoor, and Hoogley, and the Ganges, to meet its kindred rays breaking eastward from Europe; and mingling with the light of Trade and Letters, converging on the East, and the mission posts of Christianity, will kindle into a constellation that shall proclaim the cross triumphant over the crescent and every other opposing power. Is it not written in the books of Providence, that, if as patriots philanthropists, and Christians, you would regenerate the great eastern world with its millions of human beings, you must first fill this Pacific coast with an enlightened, educated, and pious population? The great world fact of the passing year is the wedding of the two great oceans of our globe. Never before on this planet was there ever celebrated so sublime a bridal. The nuptial ring that binds the rough old Atlantic to the fair Pacific is of wrought iron—significant of the indissoluble bonds that now bind two willing hemispheres. The dowry is to all nations, and consists of the millions of treasure, and of the precious things of the earth, that are to flow through this union henceforth in unremitting streams to and fro over the globe.

Another wedding, and in high life, is soon to take place. The bands are already published. Lord Shanghai is soon to lead to the altar the blooming daughter of the Pacific. The enchasings of the wedding ring now making, are to be surpassingly rich, and significant of the glowing ardor of the young couple. And I have only to wish that Miss California's rich old uncle would hasten the wedding, and that we may all be there. Meanwhile it is our privilege to hear the epithalamium in praise of the bride and bridegroom from the poet laureate.*

* Poem followed by Hon. Frank Soulé, editor of the *Chronicle.*

LECTURE III.

III.

SOME HINTS ON THE MORAL INFLUENCE OF THE COMMERCIAL SPIRIT OF THE AGE.*

"Assyria, Greece, Rome, Carthage, what are they?"

There is the moral of all human tales;
'Tis but the same rehearsal of the past!
First freedom and then glory—when that fails,
Wealth, vice, corruption—barbarism at last.

CHILDE HAROLD.

Then westward ho! in legions, boys—
Fair Freedom's star
Points to her sunset regions, boys.

No clime so bright and beautiful
As that where sets the sun;
No land so fertile, fair, and free,
As that of WASHINGTON.

MORRIS.

YOU are aware that the sages of the great cities and empires of the old world, in the fullness of their wisdom and the brilliancy of their imagination, could not see beyond the pillars of Hercules. They sailed across the Styx long before the compass enabled Columbus to unfurl

"An eastern banner o'er the western world,
And teach mankind where future empires lay,
In these fair confines of descending day."†

* Delivered at the second Anniversary of the Mercantile Library Association, of San Francisco, January 25, 1855.

† Barlow.

Columbia's early bard was more prophet than poet, in writing of empires in the future of these climes of "descending day." And "westering still," says another poet of a later day; but I beg pardon for quoting so much poetry, I will leave that to the poet of the evening, my honorable friend here on my left.* Well, prose or poetry, "westering still" is the star that leads

"The new world in its train,"

and *westward* will the stream of humanity, in its best forms, continue to flow, and it may be, sometimes, with the gush of a cataract, until it shall run *eastward* and the circle be complete.

As citizens of public spirit, you desire to see the physical resources and wealth of the country developed, and for this purpose you are constantly urging the erection of railroads and telegraph lines. You are striving to facilitate emigration by having a road across the mountains, and the great plains opened and safe for the wagon and children of the hardy pioneer. These, and a thousand other appliances for bringing out the resources of the country are all right; they are to be commended. But it is my purpose, now, to look in a brief and simple manner at the MORAL INFLUENCE OF THE COMMERCIAL SPIRIT OF OUR AGE.

* Hon. F. S. Soulé.

The subject at once commends itself to you, both as a subject of history and of experience. It is too great, however, for me to attempt any thing more than to suggest hints, and of them only such as relate to national experience. Every one of you must feel that our commercial relations are interwoven with the very framework of our national existence.

The history of free cities, and of the commerce of nations, is now receiving more attention than at any former period, but our language is still shamefully poor in its contributions to this subject. The history of commerce is a most interesting one, because of its great antiquity, for as soon as men learned the difference between *meum* and *tuum*, which was doubtless very near the beginning of their existence, they began to bully, barter, swap, and exchange, *meum* for *tuum*, with the hope of obtaining both. The history of human migrations, which is essentially connected with the commerce of nations, is also interesting to every one that studies the progress and destiny of mankind. The migrations and traffic of nations are developments of national mind. It is as the national mind is awakened and enlightened and directed toward utility, that the schemes of commerce are apprehended; in the mind of a nation are all the springs of its activity; as we trace, therefore, the outgoings of commerce, we see the progress of mind. The progressive power of a nation is always in proportion to its progressiveness of mind; the extension of a nation's commerce is, therefore, evidence of its growth, both in intelligence and in the development of its resources. We must guard against the idea, however, that our commercial greatness can be segregated from our mechanical skill or agricultural power. This can not be done. Commerce is nothing without the products of the farm, and the manufactory. Commerce and agriculture are joined together by the Creator through the mechanic. Not a single vessel can go to sea without the aid of the stalwart "tiller of the ground," and the handicraft of the knight of tools. The oaks, and pines, and hemp, without which the carpenter can not build the ship, and the products which make the ship's cargo, are all to come from the farmer's soil.

"Our commerce and agriculture, like the twins of Hippocrates, must flourish or must die together; one can not exist and prosper without the other. The lords of the sea will be strongest when the lords of the soil are most honored."

In modern times no nation can be truly great without a powerfully awakened mind and opportunities for the development of its national resources; millions of sinews, muscles, bones, and heads; thousands of bays, harbors, rivers, and lakes; millions of millions of treasure in coal and lead, and in the precious metals; the savannas and the sierras; the forests and all the wealth that lies undeveloped in the soils and streams of a continent, are nothing without mind to bring it out and to place it before mankind, so as to increase the influence of the nation. The produce of the soil, the products of the mills, and the wares of the shop, and the riches of the mines are *exponents* of the activity and skill of the national mind. As it was the Creator's design for man to labor, to till the earth and subdue it, and have dominion over it, so it was, doubtless the Divine intention that men should trade one with another, and this divine beneficent intention is the MAGNA CHARTA of human progress; and every contribution obtained from air and water, from the ocean and the clouds, from chemistry and geology, to the advancement of human science and art, is a fulfillment of the Divine mind in giving man dominion over the earth. The commerce of nations is evidently, then, agreeable to the Great Father of all; it is one of Heaven's approved agencies for overcoming the barbarism of the savage, and for elevating the moral feelings of the civilized. It is by diffusion and reciprocation that the necessities of our race are to be supplied. The Creator has wrought into the soil of the globe a capacity to feed all its tenantry; the overplus of one portion in any article of consumption is evidently intended for the deficiency of another portion, and the transfer of such commodities is left to the industry and intelligence of the human family. It is thus that the Creator has given to every unit of the human family a specific part to do for the well-being of himself, and through his individual well-being to promote the well-being of the whole race. The object of commerce is not to enable one man to live from the misfortunes of another; not to enable one man by his wits to overreach another, and live on his brother's losses. The legitimate object of commerce is to meet the necessities of one part of mankind, by supplying them with the over supplies of another part. If there are wrongs perpetrated, and evils connected with the extension of commerce, they are chargeable to its abuse, and not to its legitimate fruits; its blessings far transcend its evils; they are as the stars of the firmament, while its evils are but fire-flies in the swamps, or fire-damps in the mines. It is not the fault of commerce that some are left in want, and some are defrauded in trade; this is owing to the clogs that human depravity has fastened to its wheels. "It is man's inhumanity to man," and not any of the Creator's laws, "that has made countless thousands mourn."

The laws of commerce are good. It is only when the moral sense is blunted, that the friction of its vast machinery is dangerous. The real basis then of the commerce of nations may be, as it has well been styled, the *mutuality of self-interest.** By this is not meant selfishness. For the moral evil of self-interest is neutralized in a pure commerce by its mutuality, and "every man engaged in commerce, whether he knows it or not, consents to this mutuality of self-interest;" that is, while he honestly watches over his own interests, he allows and expects his neighbor to do the same thing, and so long as honorable principles govern men's actions, the *self-interest* of trade is kept from degenerating *into selfishness.* The importance of rightly understanding this point may be illustrated by a comparison suggested by another, and which he uses on a kindred subject: suppose, which is necessary to the very existence of commerce, that there is a common stock for human subsistence and well-being, and that this common stock is represented by a reservoir, which contains the water that is to refresh and nourish the vast population of the city, and that each individual in the city needing supplies from the reservoir is equally interested in maintaining its embankments in strength, and its waters healthful. Now, it is evident, that the well-being of the aggregate of the city's population is dependent on the faithfulness of each individual to the performance of his individual duty, in keeping up the embankments, and in watching over the purity of its waters. Now suppose that this reservoir represents the

* By Rev. Dr. Fisk of England. See his lecture.

common stock of America and of all the nations with which she trades; and again, that the United States and each nation she trades with has its own reservoir, and that each individual of each nation is intrusted with a specific duty, in reference to the keeping up of the embankments, and the preservation of the purity of the water, and you can not fail to see how each individual in the United States, and in every nation we trade with, is interested in the individual honesty and skill of every farmer, artisan, banker, tradesman, and sailor, engaged in all these nations.

And what but intelligence can keep up the embankments and keep the water pure? I am sure the history of mankind will show that those nations that are the most pure in their principles, are the greatest in their power and glory. *Commercial extension is in proportion to the prevalence of Christian intelligence and integrity.* And additional importance is affixed to this part of our subject when we consider that the age of barter in shells, hides, animals, stone, and such-like things, has given place to an age remarkable for a circulating medium, called money, consisting of precious metals, and that, on this basis, credit has become as available as money. On this point, I will not say much, for it is in the line of my friend of the "Flush Times of Alabama," who is also to address you.*

* J. G. Baldwin, Esq.

The abuses of credit have been, and may be great, but the exigences of commerce require it. Public credit is, and must be coined and stamped with the die of public approbation, in such a form as to make capital as available as the actual presence in force of the precious metals. The commerce of nations can not now be carried on without express-offices and bills of exchange; but what is commercial credit without moral worth? It is by confidence in the honesty of those engaged in banks and trade, that capital becomes as available as the precious metals themselves. But what stability can there be in such momentous transactions—transactions that stretch round the circumference of our globe, and require, even with the facilities of travel that we now have, almost a year to bring a bill of exchange home, without abiding moral principles? And I am happy to say, and from some little personal experience in different quarters of the globe, that the mercantile honesty of Great Britain, the reliability of her merchants, is one of the mightiest bands of her strength. The continentals may affect to despise her as a "nation of shopkeepers," and attempt to rival her in arms and in arts, but they are compelled both to love and fear her for her commercial integrity. I am not speaking of the haughty aristocracy, nor of the government of Great Britain, nor of her huge, imperial monopolies, but of her private bankers, manufacturers, and merchants. It is to their credit more than to her prowess in arms, great as it is, or to the gold in the vaults of her bank, that she owes her greatness; and the way for us to extend our commercial power, is to make our flag the herald ensign of national integrity. When heathen nations learn that the word of an American skipper is equal to an oath, and the promise of our merchantmen sacred as a covenant, then will they open their hearts and their treasures to us. We must gain their confidence by mildness, forbearance, firmness and truth. The interflexions of commercial life are so numerous and so vast, that, like the nervous system of the human body, you can not touch one nerve without having a response from all. The individual and aggregate well-doing of all commercial nations is, therefore, the necessary basis of their individual and aggregate well-being. The dishonesty of the artisan in making a clock, or of the weaver in making a print, of the weigher or measurer, or of the clerk, shipper, consignee, vendor, or banker, affects the whole transaction from the inception of the design of the fabric to its consumption, and is reflected back in the product of the consumer, by which the article in question was purchased; and there is as much dishonesty in the consumer, who wishes to purchase an article below its value, as there is in a vendor who sells it for more than its worth; and the dishonesty of the purchaser who wishes to get an article for less than it can be honestly afforded at, leads the artisan to make a cheap article that will resemble the high-priced one, and to sell the inferior article as the high-priced one to such customers as are not familiar with the qualities and value of such things. It is evident that the *moral spirit* of commerce is a subject that interests, not only the CONSCIENCE and the soul, both here and hereafter, but is also deeply connected with the progress and success of commerce itself; it is not merely a moral habitude that gives intensity and coloring to an existence in a state of endless retribution, but it is necessarily interwoven with success in business, and still more with the enjoyment of the fruits of success in business, even in this life.

But how shall I draw a picture of the commercial spirit of our age? Whither can we fly to escape from its presence?

The "snowy cones" and green woods of Oregon, the jungles of India, the canals of China, the sands of Coromandel, the gulches of the Sierra, and the mountains of Africa, are witnesses of its adventures, failures, and successes. I know not that there is a sea on which our ships do not float, nor a wind that does not unfurl our flag, nor a haven, upon earth, into which our merchants do not send their vessels, nor a nation on the globe with which we do not transact business. The goings forth of our commerce have covered the Atlantic with our sails, and while the Great Powers of Europe are measuring their strength for mutual destruction, to gain an ascendency over the little bright blue Mediterranean sea, it is ours to make the vast Pacific an American "lake."

The *Westminster Review* rather piquantly admits, that "cousin Jonathan does a vast stroke of actual work in the practical way; preparing the wilderness for the use of man; transforming things unowned into property, and European pauperism into American prosperity." "A very respectable, useful, and valuable relative, indeed," of his English uncle. "Altogether modern, and with a history of only two short chapters—Puritanism and Revolution"—we are nevertheless "a remarkable family of cousins—of singular, and perhaps, the most expanding, mobile, multiplying, 'go-a-head' human creatures that ever 'exploited' this terrestrial globe. * * * Hardly more settled than the halt of the exploring traveler whose night's rest is hurried and feverish with onward thoughts for to-morrow; *our* keen faculties and energies are all set on 'progress'—working for times that are not, but will be—for a Future that is to 'beat all creation.'"

And even the London *Daily News* finds time amid its pictures to say, "To watch the spirit of American commerce is to witness some of the finest romance of our times." The equator and the poles, the mountain passes and desert oases, the forest, lake, and waterfall, the sunny South and Arctic snows are as familiar to our traders and explorers as of any other nation. In traffic ours are the pearls of the South, "with birds of bright plumage," the gums and the sweets, and the spices and tea, of the East, and the gold, and silver, and gems of the New World. Our Salem rivals the fame of the Hanse-Towns, and of old Venice, the bridegroom of the sea, that has been dead and hearsed many a year. But the spirits of the Adriatic Queen have already witnessed the nuptials of the beautiful Pacific with her bridegroom of the Golden Gate. And brilliant is the wedding, and numerous as the stars will be the offspring, when Santa Claus shall come sailing in steam vessels, and riding on iron horses to pour the *bonbons* of both the East and West into her lap on Christmas Eve.

In sober reality our merchant princes are the aristocracy of Neptune; the lords of the sea. Their scepter is the trident of the floods, and the ocean's waves are their baronial acres.

In our harbors we see ships of the most distant nations riding safely. Pactolian streams literally flow into our lap; and we are in a fair way to gain the lion's share of the wealth of the world. Many of our ships carry the treasures of kings, or sufficient wealth to have founded an empire, or have created a new dynasty. Every day witnesses something contributive to our resources and mercantile power. And when we consider the shipping connected with the outlet of the St. Lawrence, the Hudson, the Chesapeake, the Mississippi and San Francisco, and anticipate the day when our valleys and mountains, from the Northern Lakes and the Eastern Atlantic to the Pacific, shall be reticulated by railroads, and filled with prosperous villages and cities, and farms and manufactories, and bound into one web of affection, and reciprocal advantage, and of Christian principle, we can not refrain from uttering the great Statesman's prayer: THAT WE MAY EVER BE ONE PEOPLE, WITH ONE CONSTITUTION AND ONE DESTINY.

What, but the urgencies of the commercial spirit could have enacted the neutrality laws now existing between us and the belligerent powers of Europe? The treaties now between the United States and Russia, and the other great nations, are an acknowledgment of the power of our commerce. The magnitude of our commercial interests, I am not able to set before you in detail. The reports of the Secretary of the Treasury and of the Census Bureau are in your hands; our tonnage and marine transactions are equal to the greatest, and superior to that of any other nation, with, perhaps, one exception. The mightiness of our commercial interests, the magnitude and extent of our mercantile operations far surpass the expectations of our forefathers, and just in the proportion of their greatness, is there danger in them involving our interests. But vast as are our commercial transactions, the spirit that is in them, is still *progressive and aggressive.* You know that the great weight of a body once in motion on an inclined plane increases its velocity, and that its progress is accelerated with every revolution of the wheel. In proportion, then, to the magnitude of the commerce of our nation, and the number and power of the various facilities by which it can be increased, will be the rapidity and force of the progress which it makes. The spirit that broods over the workshop, the plow, the loom, the ledger, and the bank, cry out for progress; there is a cry for the extension of the area of trade, whether there is for the widening of "the area of freedom" or not. In every mail that brings the news that some improvement has been made in ship-building, in agriculture, in railroads, telegraphs, and steamships, or that some new port is open to trade, some new mine discovered, or some invention made, by which elements and things already known can be turned to account; in every breeze that fills the sails of the clipper, and in the lashing of the restless waves of the great ocean at our gate, there is a loud voice calling for progress, saying to us, from the nations beyond, "Come over and help us"—and we are going; we have already gone. Loo Choo and Niphon bay have saluted American keels, and the waters of Jeddo itself have fondly embraced "the Lady Pierce."* And one of the necessary results of this vast

* American ship, Captain Burrows.

increase of mercantile pursuits IS A POWERFUL AWAKENING OF THE HUMAN MIND.

Every improvement in manufacturing, or discovery in agricultural chemistry, and every new channel that is opened up for trade, is a stimulus to human activity. The whistle of the steam-car, and the click of the telegraphic key have not only awakened old Rip Van Winkle from his sleep of ages, but have created in his history an era of new and terrible thinking, where there was scarcely a thought before. The old order of society is disintegrating everywhere; everywhere cracking and crumbling to pieces. The vast armies of Europe are but police forces to preserve order among those very refined and well behaved people called kings and emperors, and their families. The current of men's thoughts is quickened; the old tread-mill round of business is forsaken; the circle of knowledge is enlarged; the field of vision extended, and the mind awakened to the idea, to the possibility, to the actual effort of achievement; and the world has yet to see what the product will be on these glorious shores of the Pacific, of Anglo-Saxon blood warming and multiplying in an Asiatic climate. The poetry, the dreaming enthusiasm of the East, is here in living contact with the eternal activity and courage of the descendants of the followers of the Odin religion, converted to Christianity. Our blood through Cromwell and Luther runs up to the aspirants for Valhal. The Anglo-Saxon is here for the first time since the primeval emigrations from Asia westward, on a soil and under such stars and sunshine, and in the face of such hills, and mountains, and oceans, as have heretofore been identified with the developments of Oriental mind. Who can tell what will be the progeny of the blood of the heroes of Western Europe, flowing in the veins of freemen, under the mighty stimulus of republican institutions, and warmed by a Syrian sun, and fanned with breezes like those of the sacred mountains? The generations to grow up here under the ministry of life and joy from the ocean air and mountain skies, and watched over by such a galaxy of stars, and playing by springs like those of Siloa and Jordan, and wandering in valleys like those of Sharon and Esdraelon, and gazing on mountains like Lebanon and Carmel, must be generations of deep and pious thinking, and high and noble daring; and if I could say it without interrupting my thread of discourse, I would say positively, that there is no climate in Italy, or on the Mediterranean, equal to that of this State.

Another result of the expansion of commerce is a liberalizing of our views.—Just in the proportion that we are well acquainted with other nations, will our prejudices and dogged notions be removed. "Every body and his wife" now travels and trades, and in the hard jostlings of the dusty thoroughfare many of the sharp corners of humanity are rubbed off. The inhabitants of such countries, as of China and Japan, that are the most closely shut up against intercourse with other countries, are the most bigoted and narrow-minded, and filled with the idea of their superiority to other nations. But as "the John's" and "John Bulls" and "Jonathan's" and the F. F's of the "Old Dominion" travel abroad, and see the world, they become more and more tolerant and kindly disposed, and at last begin to feel that there may be, after all, some other country beside their own on the globe. As there are many beautiful objects in nature that we do not admire, because we do not see them, we are ignorant of them, so there are good and great people in all nations that we do not love, because we are not acquainted with them. Intercourse with mankind must, therefore, *liberalize* our views and remove many of our prejudices. In this point of view, the Congress of Nations at the World's Fair, where the various improvements in the modes of agriculture, methods of education, and uses of the mechanical arts were exhibited, did much good. And as the knowledge of different nations is mutually extended, so may they be bound together in bonds of mutual respect, affection and interest. Every ship that plows her way from this port to the seas of the Flowery Kingdom, is a chain that draws the two continents nearer and nearer to one another. Every new trail of the hunter over the mountains; every new path *blazed* through the forest by the buckskinned pioneer to his log cabin on the hill side, and every sod that is turned up by the spade or the plow, and every stream that is harnessed and put to work at the mill, and every railroad and telegraph wire that is stretched across this great continent, is a band of iron binding the different races and portions thereof more firmly together.

Among the dangers growing out of, and in some measure inseparable from the amplitude of our commercial transactions, are RECKLESS SPECULATIONS. Men are now found who play with ships, land lots, and "water lots" that can not be confined by stakes, and ingots of gold, as with dice; invoices, rents and commissions are staked at the gambling table, and even legitimate business is pursued as a game of chance. And of near a-kin to this demoralizing speculation, is the tendency of the day to bring down every thing to the level of the market. The Rule of Faith on 'change is the *Rule of Three*, and the Rule of Practice is—*will it pay?*

ANOTHER DANGER IS THE TOTAL ABSORPTION OF THE FINEST AND BEST FEELINGS IN A COLD AND NARROW SELFISHNESS.—It is a natural law of the mind, that in proportion to the strength with which it is fixed upon any one object, it will be drawn from all other objects. There is danger then that the mind, absorbed in the magnitude and progressiveness of commerce, will be withdrawn too much from higher and nobler things. The claims of God and man, of body and soul, of family and society, are too often neglected through an intense application to business. Perhaps such men think or say—this is true; but we can not help it; it must be so. The vessel is to be steered over dangerous seas and threatening rocks, and under the lowering clouds that may break over it at any moment. The pilot must, therefore, ever be at the helm. This may be so sometimes. But is it not often allowed to interfere with the improvement of the mind and heart when there is no absolute necessity for it? Is it not the making haste to be rich, that dares not look up to heaven, and dares not take time to bend the knee in fervent supplications for divine blessings, rather than the pursuits of a legitimate and well regulated commerce that absorbs the mind and draws it from mental and social recreations? Would it not be a gain to your families and to society, and to business in general, if there was more reading, and more domestic enjoyment among merchants and business men? Would it not be a great guide to healthfulness both of body and heart, if the mind were more perfectly drawn from the trammels of office, and allowed to escape to the library and the picture-gallery, or to enjoy the sweetness of domestic repose? There is great danger of mental contraction in our day. The horizon of some men's minds is so fearfully knit together at the corners by rent-rolls, per cents., and deposits, that they live and move and have their entire being in a hogshead, a ship, a house, or a bag of gold. Several thousand of such souls may be baled up in a single package, and leave sufficient room to breathe. So intently and strongly do they gaze upon their gains, that while they have no range without, and never lift a telescope to the glories of the vast Universe, they resort to the microscope to see how fast the grains increase their "pile." Multitudes of men, who might with proper mental, moral, and social discipline, have grasped the world of science, and the wealth of history, and "walked in the starry way of intelligence, and have gone up to the highest places of spiritual enjoyment," are groveling like worms in the dust, and in a circle of exceedingly small dimensions. They turn their meals into seasons of calculation, and their homes into counting-houses. So terrible is the despotism of the heart once yielded to the love of money, that there are not wanting some who would blast down Mount Sinai for lime or for a railroad track, if its stock could be made to pay ten per cent. O! there is terrible injustice and cruelty upon the father of a family, who allows his business to rob them of what is beyond the price of all merchandise—high moral culture and religious elevation. What if a man does gain wealth for his children, and go down to the grave with the approbation of his fellow-citizens as a successful, honest merchant, and still leaves them without a *mental* or *moral* capacity to profit by it, and to enjoy or do good with his wealth? The case is a painful one, but it is often seen. The absorbed father with his heart and mind filled with the objects and affairs of every day, returns late, wearied and worn, yet anxious for the morrow, and utterly unfit for the holy duties of his office as the head and priest of his household. The rest of the Sabbath comes in vain. The exhaustion of the week hangs over it, so that it is not a day of recreation or improvement, much less a foretaste of that rest which remaineth for the people of God. The commercial spirit of our day is so incessant, so unrelaxing in its demands upon mind, time, and strength, that it cuts off opportunities and even strength for the proper consideration of higher objects. Now, fellow-citizens, it is with such views of commerce, its mighty influence and the progress of mind of which it is both a fruit and an exponent, and at the same time aware of the dangerous tendency of the absorbing, ubiquitous spirit of trade in our day, that wise and good men in this and other cities have established Mercantile Library Associations, and have sought to awaken attention to the high morals of commerce, and to diffuse intelligence and sound principles among the masses of men engaged in trade. It is chiefly owing to the efforts of the agents, committees, lectures, and publications of such institutions in Great Britain, that the hours of business have been so shortened as to give young men employed in manufactures and counting-houses opportunities for repose, for instruction, and for moral and religious cultivation. It is in the example of heads of business houses, in the annunciations of Chambers of Commerce, and in the lectures and libraries of Mercantile Associations that we see the power to awaken and spread abroad such a moral spirit as may elevate society, and make the gains of commerce contribute to national prosperity. The purity of the conscience of our commerce is the tower of our strength.*

The right reading of the brave old nations of yore, shows that as the idea of supernatural beings was lifted off from their minds, they became gross and stupid. "As Jupiter vanished out of their sky, conscience faded in the heart." As a sense of the presence of Divine beings and of a personal accountability hereafter for the deeds of this life became feeble, and a dull and dreary Atheistic night shut down on their vision, so their energies died out and the darkness of falsehood and of ignorance settled over them in terrible gloominess. Kings may confederate and sow the earth with dragon blood; but "God makes

* See Appendix P.

facts." And all God's facts are revelations speaking of a glorious future for man. Happy the day, when commerce that swings the great hammer—"the Miollnir of Thor"—shall have broken the mountains of tyranny to pieces; and when the spirit of commerce, itself, and the toiling of the field, shop, and mill, shall be baptized into the spirit of Peace. Then will the iron of the mountains be beaten into railroads and plows, and not into muskets, shells, and sabers; and our great ships shall be the messengers of plenty and joy, and not be the floating batteries of death and woe. Happy the day when on earth's every high place, the Janus temple of the Cross shall point its soiled, dust-worn and weary millions to glory and immortality, and the din of our great cities shall be mingled with the holy music of the Gospel.

The nature of our population and our local influences, render such an Institution as this, more important to us, perhaps, than to any other city in the world. A large proportion of our population are young men who have some knowledge of the world and of books—young men of enterprise and noble daring—who are just entering upon the active pursuits of life, far away from home influences, and often placed under strong temptations to vice. This Association throws open to them its doors and its thousands of selected volumes. It is intended to continue their education which was begun at home—to cultivate the mind, and so elevate the heart that it will scorn vice and bear misfortunes.

In the libraries of this Society, they will find friends that no adversity can alienate and gain ornaments for society more precious than rubies. Here the *young man from home* may find solace in a weary hour, and acquire knowledge, that will dissipate prejudice, overthrow superstitious fears, chasten vice, guide virtue, and give grace and government to genius. In building up, therefore, this useful and noble Institution, you throw around young men, at a most critical period of their lives, the example of intelligent, and high moral business men; and you promote harmony and good feeling among citizens, and contribute to elevate the standard of public morals.

APPENDIX.

APPENDIX A.—PAGE 28.

THE ARMY OF THE WAREHOUSE.

"Lord Stafford mines for coal and salt;
The Duke of Norfolk deals in malt,
And the Douglass in red herrings."

HALLECK.

The lords of the mill, of the mines, and of the counting-room, now build castles, and sway a scepter more powerful than that of the old baronial halls. Feudalism has paled before king cotton and the steam engine. It is at the Bourse, or on the Exchange, that war is declared, or peace concluded. In the Chronicles of England, just before the passage of the Reform Bill, it is written:

"The Duke of Wellington was quite prepared with Scotch Greys, with rough-ground swords and the like, to bolster up the abuses of the Church and State; he was prepared to make the Bank bristle with bayonets, and repel any attack on it with armed bands; but men began to present checks in undue abundance, and ask for gold in exchange for notes. Frightened Directors told the Duke that the Bank could not stand the monetary siege twenty-four hours longer; and the old soldier, finding that there were powers in society not dreamed of in his gunpowder philosophy, saw immediately that he must give way to more pacific counsels."

APPENDIX B.—PAGE 44.

REPUBLICS AND LETTERS.

"It would seem," says Dr. Vaughan, in his volume on great cities, "to be the notion of some men that where there is no high hereditary class, possessing large hereditary wealth, there can be no successful cultivation of art, or of intelligence of any kind, in their higher forms. But the slightest acquaintance with the history of ancient Greece should have sufficed to prevent such an error. It may well be doubted, if the world would hitherto have seen such an age as that of Augustus, or that of Louis XIV., if it had not previously seen the age of Pericles. It is a remarkable fact, and one which the class of persons adverted to would do well to consider, that the States of Greece, which knew nothing of hereditary distinctions, which were not possessed of large wealth, which consisted of so many city communities, and were pervaded generally by the spirit of Republicanism, colonization, and commerce—that it was given to those states to supply, to all subsequent time, the highest models of the wonderful in science and art, models which the proudest empires have done well to imitate, which they have rarely equaled, and never surpassed." P. 133.

Dr. Vaughan is an Englishman, and can not be supposed to be prejudiced in favor of republican institutions.

He is one of the ablest writers of Great Britain. His work on cities is worthy of attention from all who seek information as to their influence on the various departments of human industry. But it is not only in Greece that we find a Republic the home and patron of Letters and of the Fine Arts. CARTHAGE, PALMYRA, and ROME in her greatest power, as well as ATHENS, were Republics. And FLORENCE rose out of the wreck of the dark ages essentially a republican city. It became distinguished as the home of rich traders and manufacturers, as well as the asylum of the arts. The extraordinary wealth of the Florentines flowed from their numerous manufactures at home, and their trade and banking speculations carried on by their merchants abroad. Their most important manufactures were in silks, woolens, and jewelry. Every citizen, to be eligible to office, was required to have his name on the rolls of one or other of the Trades. DANTE had his name put down as an apothecary, but he never practiced his profession. And so numerous were the influential traders of Florence residing abroad, that when Pope Boniface VIII., after his election, received the congratulatory addresses of foreign states, twelve of the envoys accredited to him, were citizens of Florence; on which Boniface exclaimed, "The Florentines constitute the fifth element of creation!" And Roscoe says, "The freedom of the Italian governments, and particularly that of Florence, gave to the human faculties their full energies." It was in their cities, the labors of the painter and the statuary were early associated with the mysteries of religion as it then prevailed, and the wealth and ostentation of individuals and of states, held out rewards sufficient to excite the endeavors even of the phlegmatic and the indolent. And in our day, where, but among our trading cities can we find a Florence? And who but our merchant princes are our Medici? Where were our benevolent enterprises, and our schools, asylums, libraries and universities, but for our Perkinses, Lawrences, and commercial benefactors?

It has been well said by Roscoe "that those periods of time which have been most favorable to the progress of Letters and Science have generally been distinguished by an equal proficiency in the arts." (Life of Lorenzo de Medici, p. 306.)

The revival of letters, arts, and commerce, was cotemporaneous in Italy. They are still respectively cause and effect. Nor can any one of the great branches of human art or industry flourish segregated from the rest.

APPENDIX C.—PAGE 64.

COMMERCE CONQUERING.

"——Whose sounding
O'er the whole earth is echoing and rebounding."
MORGANTE MAGGIORE.

BAYARD TAYLOR tells us that our national airs are heard in the jungles of India and on the slopes of the Himmalayas. There is not a nook or corner of Asia or Africa, and but few, if any, of the remote islands of the sea, where the traveler does not now find the manufactured goods of Europe and America. One of the great distinctive features of our day is the goings forth of the trade of Christian nations. And its influence in elevating society and supplying human wants justly entitles it to its pre-eminence. Compared with a *recent* past, the present attainments of human industry are an astonishing spectacle. But what are the highest conquests of the present to those of the rapidly coming future? The progress of coming years will be in geometrical ratio. The day of discoveries and inventions is by no means past. There is a great future still before the Church on earth, and for our race on this planet. BRISBANE, in a letter to the Earl of Derby, in Lingard, the Roman Catholic historian of England, says, "that the trade of England in the reign of Charles II. was at such a height that it is as hard to think it can continue so, as it was to believe once it would ever rise to it." Think of the trade of England under Charles II. and her Majesty Queen Victoria! What would Brisbane think could he write a letter now to the present Earl of Derby about clipper ships and steamers? The progress made now in seven years in all the industrial departments of the great Protestant nations of the earth exceeds that of any previous period of the same duration; and I fancy, whether our physical constitution changes every seven years or not, that great changes will take place in the affairs of the world as often as once in every seven years henceforward, and I hope always for the advance of truth. If we may judge from the history of America and Australia, all savage nations will become extinct. Wealth will prevail over the destitute. The commercial races will always succeed at last in buying out or conquering their savage neighbors. No other issue is possible, unless they adopt the arts of their trading and conquering neighbors. The savage races in contact with the civilized must submit, either to be swept away, or adopt the arts of civilization.

APPENDIX D.—PAGE 64.

THE CRADLE OF OUR RACE.

IN view of the theories put forth in our day by some of our savans, it may be of use to remember what eminent European scholars have said on the origin of the human races.

HEEREN tells us explicitly that Central Asia "from the earliest times has been regarded as the magazine of our race. And the further back we go into the history of the first ages of the world, the more probable does it appear that the whole of Western Europe received its population from thence" (Central Asia).*

And in many other places in his volumes of "Historical Researches into the Politics, Intercourse, and Trade, of the Principal Nations of Antiquity," does this great historian and profound scholar express his opinion that the interior of Central Asia is the place whence, both east and west, the human races were dispersed. It is a singular fact that as far as any traditions are known to exist among the aborigines of this continent and the far east, that they all agree substantially in claiming their origin from the same portion of the globe. And history points us with unerring certainty to the fact, that great periodical emigrations of tribes and nations have taken place from east to west,

* Heeren's Asiatic Nations, vol ii., p. 4.

and from Central Asia to the further East. It was national pride that caused some of the ancients to call themselves *autocthones*, or natives of their soil, for their national traditions and histories testified to the contrary. And if it be admitted that it is in India and Egypt that we find man first advanced in civilization—that we first find extraordinary progress in science and architecture, agriculture, and in laws and in judicial proceedings, it only proves that there man first established himself under such favorable circumstances as enabled him to develop his mental faculties in the useful and elegant arts. Dr. Latham, in his work, "Man and his Migrations," and in his larger work, "The Natural History of the Varieties of Man," substantially sustains these views. And Colonel Smith says:

"There is constantly a record of antecedent existence, though not a history, among early nations. It is variously told, but not the less the same in substance, in both hemispheres, and in the South Sea islands. Although in Central Asia, no very distinct evidence of a general diluvian action, so late as to involve the fate of many nations, can be detected, still there can not be a doubt that, with scarce an opposable circumstance, *all man's historical dogmatical knowledge and traditionary records, all his acquirements, inventions, and domestic possessions, point to that locality, as connected with a great cataclysis, and as the scene where human development took its first most evident distribution. West of central Asia, all records agree in pointing to the East for the direction whence nations migrated.*"*

It is a singular coincidence also, as to man's primeval

* Lieutenant Colonel Charles Hamilton Smith's Natural History of the Human Species, pp. 109, 110, 218.

location, that all "our historical dogmatic knowledge and traditionary records" not only as to man himself, but also as to the source of the animals, fruits, birds, and inventions that have accompanied him in his migrations, should all point to the same locality. The animals subdued for household purposes—like the dog, ox, ass, camel and horse, sheep and goats, and birds, and fruit-bearing trees and shrubs, and the wheat and barley of our fields—should all historically and by tradition point to Central Asia as the place where they were first domesticated, and whence they have been dispersed over the globe. "Even the LOTUS, celebrated in Egypt, was derived from some part of India." The evidence in our day has become complete, that even Egypt was connected with, and dependent on Asia, for the beginning of its colonies, and the origin of its civilization. In the monumental records of the Nile, many objects, living plants and shrubs, carefully transported for replanting, and also animals and other objects of value offered as tribute, "are evidently from an eastern region." The religion of Egypt was closely allied to that of India, though no doubt, both, after their separation, were modified by revolutions, innovations, and the successive incorporations of foreign elements. Colonel Smith informs us that the British sepoys, forming a part of General Sir R. Abercombie's expedition for the re-conquest of Egypt, "no sooner entered the ancient temples in the valley of the Nile, than they asserted their own divinities were discovered on the walls, and worshiped there accordingly. They even pointed out the Cresvaminam, or Brahmin distinguishing cord, as likewise a decoration of the painted divinities."

Appendix E.—Page 64.

CARTHAGE.

Whether Carthage was founded by Queen Dido, or by Zorus and Carchedon, is of but little concern to us. The lessons of its rise and fall are much more important. It was from the beginning a trading city, and by its trade grew to opulence and power. Its wealth was the product of mines, manufactures, trade both by land and water, and its fall was the result of avarice and wealth not employed in productive industry. Her caravans passed from the Nile to the Niger, and from the Deserts of Libya her gates were crowded with camels. Spain was to Carthage what Mexico and Peru became to Castile and Leon. While the tribes of the interior were farmers, hunters, and carriers to Carthage, she could sustain her immense army of mercenaries, but with the decline of her trade, her ability to carry on war declined also. The settlement of the Phenicians in Africa was for the purpose of trade. Being well situate, and gaining dominion over many of the normal tribes, and a footing in Sicily and Spain, Carthage soon became independent of Tyre. It is said by some that their navigation extended round the African continent, and to Iceland, and America. Their most salutary influence was on the native tribes, whom they caused to till the soil. In her day Carthage was the center of mmerce and one of the greatest cities of the world.

When she fell, all the dominion of commercial civilization over the tribes of Africa ceased, and it has so continued to our day. It is only of late years that even an attempt has been made to recover what was lost in the fall of Carthage. She was the only center of Letters and of Trade in Africa. Never celebrated, it is true, for her literature, nor was she wholly without libraries and authors. SALLUST informs us that King Hiempsal had a collection of Carthaginian historians, who furnished much valuable information about the early history of Africa.* PLINY makes mention of Juba's African Chronicles gathered from Punic, Libyan, Greek, and Latin authorities, which work however is lost. When the Romans conquered the Carthaginians they gave their libraries to their Numidian allies. But that it now appears as a chapter in a wise Providence, we could never forgive the Romans for their selfishness and cold blood in destroying Carthage. At her fall, the world lost her literature, and her colonies beyond the Pillars of Hercules were forgotten, and the key of their discoveries and extensive trade was lost for ages. Some of the causes that contributed to her fall were the means of extending trade and kind offices among mankind. We have already stated that she caused many of the nomadic tribes of northern Africa to become agriculturists, by demanding their tribute in corn. This was a great blessing to her and to them. But these tribes never loved her. They were always ready to rise in revolt on the approach of an enemy. It was a knowledge of this fact that made two Roman generals invade Africa at different times with an army of only fifteen thousand men. It was a great error in her policy not to make friends of the nations she conquered. Another cause of

* De bello Jugurtha.

her fall was the immense army of mercenaries she employed. Her great armies were composed almost entirely of foreigners. So rich was Carthage from her monopoly of trade, that at one time, almost half Africa and Europe were in the pay of this rich republic."* Libyans, Spanish, Gallic, Celtic, Greeks, Moors, Numidians, Ligurians, Italians, Campanians, and Balearic slingers were all found in their armies. At one time, in an army of seventy thousand men, there were only two thousand Carthaginians, who were the *sacred legion*, or body-guard of heavy-armed infantry for the commanding general. In one of their great sea-fights with the Romans, they employed three hundred and fifty galleys and one hundred and fifty thousand men, and the Romans three hundred and thirty galleys and one hundred and forty thousand men. By the employment of hired troops, however, the way of trade was extended. For as distant nations learned to know one another as comrades in arms, and fought as allies of Carthage, so did their gates open to Carthaginian traders. And her merchants cemented the friendship begun by national alliances. The same results followed the mingling of nations in Alexander's vast armies, and from the wars of the Crusades; and similar results will follow the alliances of the present war of the great nations of Europe, and from the "assemblage of nations at universal exhibitions of the world's industry."

The fall of Carthage was not, however, owing altogether to her hired troops, nor to the revolt of her nomadic tribes, nor to the power of her rival, Rome. The seeds of her decay were sown before this. Her decline began in two great abuses, the *sale of the highest places*, which was connected with bribery and elections, *and in the accumulation* of several high offices in the same person. These

* Heeren, Carthaginians, p. 123.

abuses led to gross corruption, centralization and factions, which destroyed the Great Republic of Africa. It was by the fierceness of party spirit fed by unscrupulous demagogues, that the republic was overthrown. A nation united in itself is unconquerable. *A brave nation can only die by suicide ;* but the most mighty are an easy prey to their enemies when the spirit of faction prevails over patriotism.

Appendix F.—Page 64.

ACCURACY OF OLD WRITERS.

It is clear from the learned labors of Heeren, supported as he is in most part by the researches of Denham, Clapperton, Lyon, Oudney, Hornemann, Gau and others more recent, or of less note, that much more credit is due to what the ancients, such as Pliny, Appian, Scylax, Strabo, Livy, Diodorus, Polybius and Herodotus, have written of Asia and Africa than has generally been supposed. And it is also clear that a much greater intercourse was carried on between the nations of antiquity, and that, in fact, they were further advanced in civilization, than has been generally allowed. There are sufficient vestiges still remaining of the commercial intercourse that once existed between the nations of the interior of Africa, to show that it must have been very great, and that their commerce was the soul of whatever life they had. The story of Bruce is well known. Once reputed the greatest of traveling liars, he is now restored to his place as a veracious historian.

Appendix G.—Page 66.

ANTIQUITY OF COMMERCE.

Sais, Thebes, Memphis, Carthage, and Alexandria have perished. Ammonium has dwindled into the insignificant Siwah, and Axum and Carthage are no more. But it was to commerce they owed their existence, their magnificence, and their splendor. And according to Heeren, Ceylon was the principal emporium of oriental trade for more than two thousand years. It is certain that in the Persian era there was an active commerce carried on between the Greek cities on the Black Sea, and all the interior of Scythia, north and east from Siberia to India. Different caravan routes were used, and cities grew up at both ends of these routes, and large dépôts were established on the way. The trade of these consisted of corn, furs, slaves and aromatics. And it is a remarkable fact, that in this era, the interior of Scythia, and of all the countries north and east of the Black Sea and by the Caspian Sea, and of the interior of north-eastern Africa was better known than in our day. The Hindoos in their most ancient works are represented as a commercial people. Their commodities were known in the markets of Phenicia, Carthage, Egypt and Babylon. In the Arabian Nights, and in the Ramayana, merchants appear as having traveled from one place to another, and all over the world, and as men possessed of liberal views high rank, and of the highest intelligence. It is the conclusion of Heeren, supported by a great many other authorities, that a regular chain of mercantile nations extended at a very remote day from China to India, and to the Black Sea, and to the nations on the Mediterranean, and also to Arabia and Egypt, through the cities of the Indus, the Euphrates, and the Red Sea. Gold was so plenty that iron was more precious. Their armor, and horses' bridle-bits were plated with it, or made of it, as also many of their vessels. This supports several allusions to gold in the Bible.

Appendix H.—Page 67.

AUSTRALIA.

The want of an indented sea margin, and the vast square mass of inland in Australia, and the barren uniformity of its scenery, or rather the want of scenery, is believed by some writers and naturalists to be the cause of the degradation of its aborigines. And the gloom of its future history is only relieved by the fact that it is now in the possession of a race who, by education and commercial energy are superior to the accidents of physical geography. These facts, if admitted as facts, and applied to us are much in our favor. We are possessed of every thing requisite to overcome any unfavorable tendencies that may exist in any part of our domain. We have a vast and variegated sea margin, inland and transmarine trade, and an endlessly variegated interior scenery.

A glance at the map of those countries distinguished for their civilization, shows that their extent of sea coast has called out their ingenuity. Sea-inlets, adjacent islands, and transmarine shores have been found favorable to enterprise and corporeal exertion. Witness "the isles of Greece" and Scotland. Facilities of intercourse are also promoted by a general proximity to the great highways of nations.

Appendix I.—Page 69.

ALEXANDER THE GREAT.

So intent was this conqueror to render the union of his subjects complete, that a tablet was found after his death, among his magnificent plans, containing a resolution to build several new cities, some in Asia, and some in Europe, and to people those in Asia with Europeans, and those in Europe with Asiatics, that by intermarriages, and exchange of good offices, the inhabitants of these two great continents might be gradually molded into a similarity of sentiments, and become attached to each other with mutual affection. (Diod. Sicul., lib. xviii.., c. 4.)

APPENDIX J.—PAGE 69.

MOHAMMED.

IT is not within the design of this little work to discuss the rise and progress of Mohammedanism, nor to settle the question as to whether Mohammed was a fanatic or a knave. Our countrymen, Dr. George Bush and Washington Irving have each written eloquently and learnedly on the life and doings of the great Arabian prophet. A few items seemed call for, however, in illustration of the remarks made in the second lecture on the trade of the Saracens or followers of Mohammed. It was as a traveler and merchant that the founder of Islamism acquired the knowledge and means to make himself a prophet. At one time in early life we find him going with his uncle Zobier with a caravan to Yemen, and then to Syria. And sometimes with the same uncle, or another one, engaged in warlike expeditions. It was, however, as a commercial agent or factor, that we find him chiefly employed. His business enlarged his sphere of observation both of men and things, and gave him a quick insight into the state of human affairs. He was also a frequenter of the great fairs held at Mecca, which were common before he preached the new faith. These fairs were not merely exhibitions of trade, but sometimes, like the games of Greece, they were also poetical contests between different tribes. Poems and other literary compositions were read, and prizes adjudged to the victors, and the prize pieces were treasured up in the archives of the city. At the fair of Ocadh seven prize poems were hung up as trophies in the CAABA. At these fairs also popular traditions were recited, and in this manner various religious faiths and the legends of the religions of remote times and distant countries were kept afloat in Arabia. And thus the trade, religion, and letters of the times were all blended together. Mohammed married the widow of a rich merchant. Her business was extensive and she required some one to manage it. Mohammed was now about twenty-five years of age, and reputed to have been possessed of extraordinary beauty and engaging manners.

It was no strange thing, therefore, that Mrs. Widow Cadijah employed him to conduct her caravans to Syria. She promised to give him double wages, and so much was she pleased with his management of her affairs, that on his return, she paid him double the amount of wages agreed on. And after sending him on several other trading expeditions to Southern Arabia, she rewarded him not only with double wages, but with herself. Now in the traditions with which Mohammed was well acquainted, Heathen, Hebrew, and Christian, and in the enlargement and quickening of his intellect by trade, and the improvement of his manners by intercourse with men, and in the power of his wealth and of his mighty connections, and the influence of his tribe, on the one hand, and in the fact that the whole world was then almost overrun with idolatry both Pagan and Christian so called, on the other hand, there seems to be no difficulty in accounting for his success in preaching the Divine unity and spirituality. Similar causes to some extent will explain the progress of Mormonism. Mormonism is not really a new religion. It has existed in all ages; and the apathy of Christendom, the deadness of the churches, the neglect of the temporal well-being of the masses by nominally Christian countries, the appeal made to the poor of Europe to better their worldly condition and gain political rights by becoming Mormons and emigrating to this country, and the natural selfishness and corruption of man are quite sufficient to account for the success of the wicked and abominable faith established in the modern Sodom on the banks of the American Dead Sea.

Appendix K.—Page 81.

GOD IN TRADE.

Providence has, in a most remarkable manner, ordained commerce, and given trade a fixed place among the laws of the universe, by conferring treasures on some portions of the earth that others have not, and displayed supreme goodness and wisdom in having so constituted the races of men that, respectively, they do not, and can not exist in the higher and best states of civilization without the mutual exchanges of the products of the different portions of the globe, and the exercise of the kind offices of good neighborhood, and reciprocal good will. "Nature compels mankind to a mutual intercourse, by endowing even the desert with articles necessary for human existence."*

Take Africa as an illustration of this remark of Heeren. Salt and dates are two great essential commodities of the Africans. But the salt pits are in the interior, where the date does not grow. And gold dust is not found where the date grows, nor where the salt is obtained. And so also we find coal and cotton usually remote from each other, and the precious metals alike remote, at least in large quantities, from both. It is thus God has distributed his bounties that men may be compelled to establish

* Heeren.

a mutual intercourse. It is thus that Providence urges man to industry, intercourse, and trade; and also indicates by the course of rivers and mountains, by estuaries and seas, and oases, the routes or channels of human intercourse. In large portions of the Old World the great routes of travel are unchangeably fixed. But for the oases of the deserts large regions of Asia and Africa must have remained forever unknown to man. But with the oases God has given man animals that can sustain great heat, carry great burdens, and perform tedious journeys without water. It is the God of all mercies who both dotted the sandy wastes with islands as resting-places for travelers, and pointed out the routes by which human intercourse shall be carried on. Hence it is that the caravans of Africa are moving along to-day the very same routes their forefathers traveled thousands of years ago. From the days of Hannibal, when Carthage monopolized the wealth of Africa, to our own, there has been but little changed in its caravan routes. The same route is pursued now between Fezzan and Upper Egypt, that the Garamantes traveled when they hunted for men. We have heard of late years a great deal of "God in Science," and "in History." This is all right enough, but why do we not hear something also of *God in Commerce?*

Appendix L.—Page 84.

CONNECTION OF TRADE AND LETTERS.

"The more the refined arts advance, the more sociable do men become; nor is it possible that, when enriched with science, and possessed of a fund of conversation, they should be contented to remain in solitude, or live with their fellow-citizens in that distant manner which is peculiar to ignorant and barbarous nations. They flock into cities; love to receive and communicate knowledge; to show their wit or their breeding; their taste in conversation or living; in clothes or furniture. Curiosity allures the wise, vanity the foolish, and pleasure both. Particular clubs and societies are everywhere formed; both sexes meet in an easy and sociable manner; and the tempers of men, as well as their behavior, refine apace. So that beside the improvement they receive from knowledge and the liberal arts, it is impossible but they must feel an increase of humanity from the very habit of conversing together, and contributing to each other's pleasure and entertainment. Thus *industry*, *knowledge*, and *humanity* are linked together by an indissoluble chain; and are found, from experience as well as reason, to be peculiar to the more polished, and what are commonly denominated the more luxurious ages." (Essay on Refinement in the Arts.)

Appendix M.—Page 90.

RISE OF POPULAR LIBERTY IN CITIES.

The history of Europe shows that with the granting of charters to cities soon after the Crusades, a new era dawned in regard to popular liberty. The enlargement of ideas consequent upon the Crusades awakened the spirit of commerce, especially in Venice, Genoa, and Pisa, and wealth flowed in such abundance into those cities that they were soon able to secure a large measure of liberty and independence. The oppression of the feudal system caused many of the cities of Europe to form themselves into communities or corporations. Dr. Robertson thinks that the granting of municipal jurisdiction to the cities of Europe as bodies politic "contributed more than any other cause to introduce regular government, police, and arts, and to diffuse them over Europe." (Charles V., View, etc., p. 19.)

But it was the advantages of commerce that first led the cities of Italy to think of shaking off the yoke of feudalism, and to establish among themselves such a free and equal government as would render property secure and industry flourishing. "The great increase of wealth which the crusades brought into Italy occasioned a new kind of fermentation and activity in the minds of the people, and excited such a general passion for liberty and independence, that before the conclusion of the last Cru-

14*

sade, all the considerable cities in that country had either purchased or had extorted large immunities from the emperor," (Ib.) The same immunities were soon extended to France and over Europe. And so jealous were the corporated cities of their liberty, that if any slave found refuge in any one of them and was not claimed for a year he was declared a freeman, and admitted as a member of the community. The immediate effects of the rise of corporated cities and of their leagues against the violence of the feudal lords, were that industry revived, and commerce began to flourish, and population increased; and wealth flowed into them; and as they became more populous and wealthy, and extended their intercourse among themselves, and into foreign countries, it became more and more necessary to adopt salutary and liberal laws, and to execute them with promptitude and integrity. The influence of liberal institutions and of polished manners in wealthy cities was of course soon insensibly diffused through the rest of society. And as their inhabitants had obtained personal freedom, and municipal jurisdiction, so they soon acquired civil liberty and political power. To the entrance of the representatives of cities into the legislatures of Europe must we ascribe the rise of popular liberty in the feudal kingdoms. They became an intermediate power between the king and the nobles, and the guardians of civil rights and privileges. "Almost all the efforts," says Robertson, "in favor of liberty in every country of Europe, have been made by the representatives of cities in their legislature." This fact is also illustrated in the rise and history of the cities that became great from the trade of the Lombards carrying the treasures of the East to the Baltic. (See the History of the Hanseatic League).

Appendix N.—Page 91.

PREJUDICE AGAINST COMMERCE.

Trade is ordained of God. Still there is a considerable prejudice against it. The Turks are strongly prejudiced against shop-keeping and tavern-keeping. The Greeks keep their hotels, and the Armenians and Jews do their customs, collecting and Bank-shaving. Many honest and hard-working people in Christian countries entertain also a kind of prejudice against merchants and traders, as if they were getting their living by their arts, rather than by their work, and not only living without work, but living off other people. It is considered a hardship to have to work to raise or manufacture articles of trade, and then that somebody else should make a living better than ours merely by selling our articles. But in the long run, it is found best there should be a division of labor and of trades, and that things should be in these matters very much as they are. Such affairs are like water, if just let alone they will regulate themselves, and find their true level.

This prejudice against trade is not confined to the ignorant. Plato taught that in a well regulated commonwealth the citizens should not engage in commerce, nor the State aim at obtaining maritime power. He contended that commerce corrupts the purity of the morals of the citizens, and the sea-service would accustom them to find so many pretexts for wrong-doing, that all military discipline would be destroyed, and every manly habit. He asserted that it would have been better for the Athenians to have continued to send annually the sons of seven of their principal citizens to be devoured by the Minotaur, than to have changed their ancient manners and have become a maritime power. Aristotle adopted the same ideas. Plato says that the capital of the perfect republic which he delineated should be situated at least ten miles from the sea. (De Legibus, lib. iv.)

Appendix O.—Page 91.

LORENZO DE MEDICI.

"Those are to be esteemed peculiarly happy, who, having improved their minds by study, can withdraw themselves at intervals from public engagements and private anxiety, and in some agreeable retreat indulge themselves in ample range through all the objects of the natural and moral world."—Roscoe's "Lorenzo de Medici," p. 67.

A word more may be allowed about this great man, to whom literature owes so much; and this the more, because in him we find a happy union of the elegant and the useful pursuits of life. We find him at the same time searching over Italy and Greece for manuscripts, and seeking to govern his own city and to preserve the peace of Italy, and to defend Christendom against the Turk. And we find him delighted in his farm and library and with his literary associates; and yet his cows were the best in the world; his stables remarkable for order and neatness; his dairy supplied Florence with cheese, so that they were no longer obliged to procure it from Lombardy; and his hogs fed by the whey from his cheese grew to a remarkable size; and his poultry-yard was graced by peacocks, and quails, and pheasants. And his gardens and orchards, and especially of mulberries, were so extensive that it was hoped the price of silk would be greatly reduced. And yet this is the man to whom we are to ascribe in a great degree the revival of a taste in Europe for the works of the ancients, and the establishment of public libraries, which in their turn became the active agents of further movements in the world of science. And thus had God ordained that when Constantinople fell, eastern science should find a home in Italy—and that as letters were flying from the cimiter of the fierce Mohammed II., there should be an asylum for them at the foot of the Alps. This is the man—this worker in mines, this overseer of farms, and this factor of goods; this swine-raising, cheese-making, garden-planting patron of letters and of the fine arts—that is represented as the father of all such as dwell in the tents of dilletantism, or dance before the glass of nambypambyism.

When the factors and correspondents of Lorenzo de Medici gave him so much trouble by their incompetence and negligence that he closed his mercantile concerns and relinquished the fluctuating advantages of commerce for the more certain revenue of his farms in Tuscany, one object he had in view was that he might enjoy more leisure for pious reading. The existence and attributes of God were favorite subjects of meditation with him. Often was he accustomed to say, "he is dead even to this life, who has no hopes of another." Often did he discourse eloquently of the insufficiency of temporal enjoyments to fill the mind, and of the probability and moral necessity of a future state.

It is difficult to define or fully conceive how much we owe to those who in past ages have been instrumental in preserving the treasures of wisdom. Such collections of manuscripts and of books as were gathered on the foundation begun by the Medici are the SENSORIUM of our race. They were torch-bearers to the great MARTIN LUTHER and his co-laborers.

APPENDIX P.—PAGE 129.

CONSCIENCE IN BUSINESS.

MR. JOHN HIGGINSON at Salem, Mass., in 1663 uttered the following potent words:

"My brethren, this is never to be forgotten, that our New England is originally a plantation of *religion*, and not a plantation of trade. Let merchants, and such as are making *cent. per cent.*, remember this. Let others who have come over since at several times, remember this, that worldly gain was not the end and design of the people of New England, but religion. And if any man among us make religion as *twelve*, and the world as *thirteen*, let such an one know he hath neither the spirit of a true New England man, nor yet of a sincere Christian." This extract is highly suggestive. It is true that New England was "originally a plantation of religion, and not a plantation of trade." "Freedom to worship God," and not gain, was the chief end of the Puritan colonists. And yet where on the face of the earth has the gain of godliness in this life been more speedily and munficently realized? It may be true now as is alleged, that we are a money-loving people —that many New England men "make religion as *twelve*, and the world as *thirteen*, but it is also true that our fathers were refugees from political and religious persecution. They were led by faith. And if some of their descendants have lost their spirit, it does not follow but that the Saviour is faithful in fulfilling his promise, that whosoever should give up houses and lands for his sake, should receive an hundredfold. There is no portion of this continent equal, in regard to actual wealth, to that settled by New England men. It is not to be inferred from this statement, that wealth is in itself inconsistent with religion, nor that the true worldly interests of a man require him to give up his piety. Without doubt a merchant's interests lie in the line of his commercial transactions. It consists in his invoices, insurances, commissions, profits, rent rolls, and bills of exchange. But is this all? Was not every merchant a man before he was a merchant? And are his interests as a man sunk in his interests as a merchant? Does the merchant's relation to his money rend asunder his relation, as a man, to virtue and society, social and domestic. Hath not God joined principle, truth, and duty to our every individuality as firmly as our immortality? The philosophy of the Bible, brought down from heaven to the counting-room, teaches, that "inside of every merchant there is, or has been, and ought still to be, 'a man.'" His circumstances may have been favorable to his integrity, or the reverse. His education, and habits, and pursuits may be varied, almost infinitely so; but in every merchant there ought still to be *a man*.

It is as short-sighted a policy in business as it is wicked in the sight of God to suppose that we may regard our conscience in dealing with our fellow-men as Frederic II. is said to have considered religion in a king. "Religion," said he, "is absolutely necessary to the well-being of States, and he is not a wise king who allows his subjects to abuse it; nevertheless, he is not a wise king who himself has any religion at all." But how does the merchant expect his clerks to be honest with him, if they see him cheating his customers? Is it reasonable for the fraudulent banker to expect his debtors to be honest to him, if he is not honest toward his creditors? In the long run, as we measure to others, it is measured to us again. "A rogue in grain becomes a rogue in spirit in every thing." It is thought, somehow or other, by some people, that to be a merchant is to pursue such a calling as endangers one's integrity. Dr. JOHNSON said, a long time ago, that "an English merchant is a newly-discovered species of gentleman"—a species that live without work. If this were ever true of English merchants, it is not true now, for merchants are now hard toilers. Another satirical Englishman, and no mean poet, COWLEY, says, "A man in much business, must either make himself out a knave, or the world will make him out a fool; and if the injury went no further than being laughed at, a wise man would content himself with retaliation; but the case is much worse, for these civil cannibals, as well as the wild ones, not only dance round such a taken stranger, but at last devour him." Now, are these derisive and severe remarks just? Do business men deserve them? I am firmly persuaded to the contrary. Or if such remarks are well-founded, merchants are themselves to blame, and to blame either because they do not recognize a proper standard in their business, or if they do, they do not live up to it. There is no necessity for wrong-doing in legitimate trade. There may be as much honesty and piety among merchants as among any other class of men. Generally they are like Jeremiah's figs. The good are very good, and the bad are very bad. In trade, as among military men, there should be a high standard of honor, and all departures from it should be visited with deserving penalties.

It is humiliating to hear so much of fraudulent failures, false swearing, and false entries, and false marking of goods, and of petty villianies. But there is still such a thing *as business honor*. It is not yet laid away with antediluvian fossils. Yet there is danger of adopting a modification of the maxim, that "honesty is the best policy." It has already been suggested that it should read, "It is not always *the best* honesty which is the best policy." For it is contended that a great merchant is made, as Lord Bacon said an eminent statesman was, by "the union of great and mean qualities." But who has written the Novum Organum, or the Principia, or the "Essay on Geographical Distribution of Right and Wrong," that demonstrates how a man may lay aside his great principles when he goes to his place of business, and put on his meanness as he does his office coat? Has any La Place discovered laws by which it is established that an act that is base and dishonorable in private life becomes legitimate on the street, or in the Exchange? A good conscience in business is the only source of perennial peace, and the more extended are our business relations, the more important it is to preserve our commercial integrity as a people.

www.ingramcontent.com/pod-product-compliance
Lightning Source LLC
LaVergne TN
LVHW021400110826
845150LV00007B/1727

* 9 7 8 1 4 2 5 5 1 3 5 0 4 *